FANTASEERS:
A BOOK OF MEMORIES

FANTASEERS:
A BOOK OF MEMORIES

Lewis Turco

Star Cloud Press
Scottsdale, Arizona

FANTASEERS:
A BOOK OF MEMORIES

Copyright © 2005
by Lewis Turco

Jacket Design by Trish Hadley

All rights reserved. No part of this book may be used
or reproduced in any manner whatsoever without written permission
from the publisher, except in the case of brief quotations
embodied in articles and reviews.

Published by

```
~ STAR CLOUD PRESS ~
```

an imprint of
Cloudbank Creations, Inc.

6137 East Mescal Street
Scottsdale, Arizona 85254-5418

ISBN: 1-932842-15-2
Paperback $ 14.95

StarCloudPress.com

Library of Congress Control Number: 2005927865

Printed in the United States of America

OTHER BOOKS BY LEWIS TURCO

The Collected Lyrics of Lewis Turco / Wesli Court, 2004
A Sheaf of Leaves: Literary Memoirs, 2004
The Book of Dialogue, 2004
The Green Maces of Autumn: Voices in an Old Maine House, 2002
The Book of Forms, Third Edition, 2000
The Book of Literary Terms, 1999
A Book of Fears ,1998
Bordello: A Portfolio of Poemprints, with George O'Connell, 1996
Emily Dickinson, Woman of Letters, 1993
The Public Poet, 1991
The Shifting Web: New and Selected Poems, 1989
The Fog: A Chamber Opera in One Act, with Walter Hekster, 1987
Visions and Revisions of American Poetry, 1986
The Compleat Melancholick, 1985
American Still Lifes, 1981
Pocoangelini: A Fantography & Other Poems, 1971
The Inhabitant, 1970
Awaken, Bells Falling: Poems 1959-1967, 1968
First Poems, 1960

Cover photo: Fantatnafs at Money Island, 1951. Photo by Howard Iwanicki. On the porch at left: Sandy Kettelhut; on the stairs, beginning at the top left: Alice Van Leuvan, Jane O'Neill, Judy Nott; bottom stair, far left: Fred Flatow, Paul Wiese; on ground, Carolyn Pearson, Charles Verba.

FOR THE FANTATNAFS
OF MERIDEN, CONNECTICUT,
WHEREVER THEY MAY OR MAY NOT BE

ACKNOWLEDGMENTS

Early versions of "Lemon Ice" first appeared in *Crosscurrents* and *The Bridge* under the titles "Lemon ice" and "The Folk," respectively. These were combined and expanded to appear as "Lemon Ice" in *Voices in Italian Americana*, and this version was reprinted in the anthology *Two Worlds Walking* edited by Diane Glancy and C. W. Truesdale for New Rivers Press in 1994.

"Father and Son" was first published in *Voices in Italian-Americana*. A version of it was originally used as the "Introductory Memoir" for *The Spiritual Autobiography of Luigi Turco*, edited for The Center for Immigration Studies at the University of Minnesota, Rudolph J. Vecoli, Director, with support from the Research Foundation of the State University of New York, all rights reserved 1969.

"Paul" was originally published in *The Bridge*.

"Nancy" was originally published in *Confrontation*.

"Burns" originally appeared in *Lake Effect*.

"Ray" was first published in *The New Review*.

"Curt" originally appeared in *The North Atlantic Review*.

"Peter the Unlucky" was first published by *River City* of the University of Memphis.

An early and much shorter version of "The Mutable Past" appeared as "Big Ed" in *Yankee*; the full version appeared in *The Virginia Quarterly Review*.

"Lemon Ice," "Mom May," "Gene and Genes" "Father and Son" and "Jean" appeared together as a chapbook, *Shaking the Family Tree*, published by Bordighera, Inc., © 1998 by Lewis Putnam Turco.

CONTENTS

Lemon Ice	1
Mom May	11
Gene and Genes	22
Father and Son	31
Curt	46
The Mutable Past	58
Paul	67
Burns	75
Pierre of Sunny Border	91
Ray	98
Nancy	108
Peter the Unlucky	115
Jean	126
About the Author	136

LEMON ICE

Pick a day, just any summer day between 1945 and 1947. The sun is boiling down through the big elm on the corner of Springdale and Windsor Avenues in Meriden, Connecticut, and Lewis is sitting on the front steps of the parsonage looking across Windsor at the run-down corner grocery store, Galluzzo's Market. If he shifts his gaze and looks right, to the northern corner, he will see another grocery — not quite so run-down, not quite so large — Cotrona's.

In the house behind Lewis his father, Luigi, is hard at work on his English and Italian language sermons for the coming Sunday. Like some scuttler of the deep, he has retreated into the sunporch behind the bookcases he's arranged in such a way as to cut himself a slice of space for his study. If Lewis were standing in the French double doorway of the porch he might watch for a moment the liquid movement of the angelfish among the valisneria in the aquaria that take up the rest of the wall space in the porch. They are Lewis's aquaria. The cries of his brother Gene, out playing somewhere with the neighborhood kids, might swim in the window: "Allee allee infree!"

Lewis's father will deliver his sermons from the pulpit of the white clapboard First Italian Baptist Church behind the house, facing Springdale, surrounded by a wire fence. It is a box of wood without even a steeple, but the churchyard is a large one — Lewis should know, he has to mow the lawn once a week. On it the church each summer holds its Strawberry Festival, the chief attraction of which is not the strawberry shortcake but the Italian pastries sold at the booths manned by large Italian women and patronized by slender Italian men and loud Italian-American children.

The church and parsonage literally and figuratively straddle the corner where Italian and German neighborhoods collide in a melee of great trees and No Parking signs. The whispers of the Roman Catholic neighborhood of Springdale have it that these renegade Protestant Italians are holy rollers. The funny little Sicilian priest had wanted to marry some Mayflower queen. They drink real blood, not grape juice, in those shot glasses. They hire a band to praise the Lord — but the band isn't hired, for Elsie plays the new Hammond and old Mr. Parisi brings his fiddle to church on special days. Somebody puffs into his trumpet, somebody else has an accordion, and the noise is always lovely.

In the days of their early childhood Lewis and his brother Gene used to swing on the church gate made of wire and silver tubing. There always seemed to be a bully around to spoil their fun and to challenge them as they rode the barrier that sealed the churchyard off from the neighborhood. "Let's see you spit on the stairs," he might dare Lewis. "You're scared, punk. Your old man eats snails. Where do you people keep the snakes you kiss on Sunday?"

Lewis's mother is somewhere indoors working on the laundry or the floors, perhaps. She is the unhappy one. A midwest farm girl who worked her way out of the fields her father let go to seed, who struggled her way through college to become a missionary among the immigrant Italians, she had married one of them and lost the status she had fought and scrambled for.

Lewis's younger brother, Gene, is lurking around somewhere, no doubt planning to horn in on whatever Lewis eventually does. What he is planning is getting over to the lemon ice store. The problem is lack of money, but Lewis believes he has solved it.

He gets up and walks slowly across the patch of green lawn under the elm, around the end of the fence at the corner, and cuts across Springdale. Inside Cotrona's it is cool and the smell is of sawdust and salami — the sawdust is sprinkled across the floor, and the salamis hang with the cheeses from wires stretched across the ceiling. There are kegs of olives in the aisle. Behind the counter stands Frank Cotrona minding the store for his father. As usual, the store is otherwise empty of customers.

"Did y' come over to go a couple rounds?" Frankie asks, grinning. Lewis nods. Frank and he are the same age, but Frank is bigger. "Same deal? Three rounds for a nickel bag of chips?" Lewis shakes his head. Frankie's smile disappears. "What, then?" He leans his elbows over the counter and looks at Lewis, his pompadour flopping over his dark eyes.

"Three rounds for a nickel," Lewis says.

"A nickel!" Frank wails and straightens up. "The priest's kid has gone pro!" His eyes are fake wide. Frankie and Lewis stand there staring at each other for a minute. "Okay," Frankie says, "it's a deal."

Frank comes around the counter untying his white apron. They square off, hands open. Frank zips one in and taps Lewis on the cheek. He laughs. "Come on, Turk, earn your money." Frank has a longer reach.

Lewis gets mad at all the little taps and goes windmilling in.

Frankie backs off laughing and defending himself. "Okay, okay, that's your round," he says. He hauls a dime out of his pocket and hands it to his sparring partner. "Six rounds, and I throw in a nickel bag of chips," he says. The match resumes.

"Thanks, Frank," Lewis says pocketing the cash at last. They shake. Frankie goes back behind the counter as Lewis goes out and closes the door behind him.

He turns left. There's a house next door on Springdale, then Ponzillo's Tavern, the bone in his father's craw, for it is almost across the street from the church. This is a place that ranks in fable in the Italian community of Springdale, but not in the mythology of the Germans and mixed breeds of Windsor. This is the house and storefront where the Gallicized Ponselle sisters were raised, the only divas Meriden ever produced. Lewis knows this, but he doesn't know why their name is Ponselle, not Ponzillo, and he has never heard them sing, for Rosa Ponselle's years of glory had been over for nearly a decade and a half. She had stopped singing at the Metropolitan in 1937, when Lewis was three years old and still living in Buffalo. Luigi loves opera, but Lewis won't listen to it when it is played on the radio or the wind-up phonograph.

Next door is the lemon ice store. "Agostino's Fish" it says on the dusty window, but Lewis has never seen a fish inside. His throat is as dry as the last leaf, and the sun is hotter than ever. He goes in, the bell on a jiggler over the door makes its Christmas sound — "Allo, boy," Mrs. Agostino says, smiling, the faint mustache over her lip arching like the back of a cat. She sits in a chair beside the ice-cream freezer, in front of the window. The candy counter is before the back wall, and behind it is the lemon ice machine: a wooden bucket containing a smaller metal vat that has a top with a gear. Over this fits another gear on a drive-wheel, the whole thing hooked to an electric motor. Ice, sugar, and lemons go inside, ice and salt go outside, the motor goes round. It is not going round now. Mr. Agostino — large, not terribly friendly — is putting together the ingredients.

It has been many years since this childless couple stepped off the boat to find the fortune to be found in an antique motor and tub, in ice, sugar, and lemons, in paper accordion cups one can squeeze the flavor out of. If you eat too fast the most excruciating headache will momentarily blind you as pain spreads through and across your sinuses. When you are done with the ache and the lemon ice you throw the cup away on the summer sidewalk outside where the kids have collected maybe to play ball or break a window or go walking down the street full of slat-frame one- or two-decker houses, some with a cat on a strip of earth looking out for the family dog through the spokes of a rusty trike between the weedy steps and the feet of passers-by, the phone poles growing their vines through the leafless breeze scuttling newsprint along the street, the grainy shingles knocked up underneath some old living room turned into a grocery store where all the cornflake boxes on the shelves host banqueting black specks that scatter in the bowl after the rustling has stopped.

"You got a lemon ice?" Lewis asks.

He is out of luck. Mrs. Agostino shakes her head. "We makin' somma now," she says, "'bout a half-hou'. You come back, eh?" Lewis stands still, deeply hurt, deeply frustrated. How can fate be so unrelenting? Mrs. Agostino understands. "You wanna Milky Way?" she asks. Lewis shakes his head and shows her his single dime. "Wella, half-hou'," she says again. "That'sa no so long."

The shadows in the shop gather heat to themselves and smother the corners of the store. In the counter only the hard candies are not in immediate danger of melting — the dots of candy on long strips of paper, the sour balls. All the rest — the jelly hats, the Baby Ruths — may not survive a half hour, no more than Lewis will. He turns to leave just as the bell rings again.

"Oh, no! What do you want?" Lewis asks. It is Gene standing in the doorway.

"Lemon ice," he says.

"They're out. Let's go." He starts to push by his brother, then stops. "Where'd you get the money?" Gene drops his eyes. "You don't have any, right?"

"Where'd you get yours?" Gene asks.

"Hey, you kids!" Mr. Agostino yells, "Closa da door. Da flies comin' in!"

Lewis grabs Gene by the arm and yanks him outside. "You never mind where I got mine," he says. "That's a secret."

"You been boxing with Frankie?"

Lewis can feel the gorge rising in his throat. It's bad enough that he's dry and hurt, now he's mad. He shoves Gene again, hard this time, hard enough to knock him down. Gene scrapes his knee and starts to cry. Lewis crosses the street, opens the church gate and latches it behind him — Gene doesn't know how to get the two halves to go back together right and get the vertical bolt to fit into the round hole in the pavement. Lewis glances back and sees Gene picking himself up and heading for the corner to cross toward the front yard. By the time he gets there Lewis will be long gone.

Lewis opens the gate again, crosses the street, and starts walking down the block along Springdale, past houses and shops, until he reaches Bonanzinga's Bakery where, if it were autumn, he could loaf on a cool day and watch the bread brown in the stone oven stoked with coal.

The loaves leave the oven on a long wooden spatula as Enrico's arms, like brown loaves themselves, move in and out among the rustlings of the narrow white bags. There is a measured bustle in the bakery. "Eh!" Enrico might say, "make some dough; make some more dough." And so they make some dough — they mix it, they knead it, they cut it, they mold it, then into the oven to bake it. Lewis buys it, hot, for a quarter — hot, for they would be waiting at home. "Go!" says Enrico, "go, run! Bread gets cold quick on a cool day."

This, though, is anything but a cool day. On days when it is very hot in the sunny streets like this and the gang languishes after lunch and the morning games, Lewis and his friends might continue down the block to Lewis Avenue, sluggish with heat, and turn left. There, parked at the curb, across the street and two storefronts down from where Lewis had lived when he was in kindergarten, would be the ice-house on wheels.

When they come to the dreamy door that roars its crystal silence into the sun; where the cubes of sawdust winter rest waiting for the fellows to pick up chips to suck; when they come to that best of quiet doors, there Guido sits with his hat pulled down, and his eyelids pulled down as well, and the shadows down, down to his knees like an awning's ghost. There is no movement, not even of his lips, as Guido says, "Welcome, boys. Come in, get cool. Get cool near the ice, boys," Guido says.

Across Lewis Avenue, on the opposite corner of Springdale, there is the establishment of Louie the barber. When Lewis was five all he had to do was cross the street cater-corner to get to the barbershop. There, Louie would lower the boom on the boys' cowlicks and locks. As Lewis walked in he'd get a snootful of pomade smells — Vitalis, Wild Root Cream Oil, Charley. He'd sit in the leather-upholstered, white porcelain, pneumatic chair, his head bent forward on his chest while Louie snipped and combed. Lewis would be thinking, perhaps, of the bats thwacking in the back lot while he sat there itching and the mirror near the chair beckoned him to move...just once.

"Well, the Yanks won," Louie would say, "yes, the Yanks won and the Sox lost. What grade you in now, sonny? Steady now, steady your head...one more swipe with the comb...wish I could comb my hair," said Louie. "See?" He'd lower his bald pate to be patted. "Bene, bene, go home now. You're done, you're ready for church tomorrow. Next man, who's next? Who's next?" asked Louie.

Lewis crosses Springdale and turns back toward home. If he stops at Tomassetti's Market about a third of the way down the block he will find Mr. Tomassetti, the father of Mario and Eddie, two kids from the church who were about Lewis's own age, spraying lambchops out from under his snickersnee as though he were some gory potentate mucking his way to empire through the limbs of his enemies.

Underfoot the going is unsteady, for the floor is covered with wood shavings that slide up to the showcases that hold a museum of meat that reminds Lewis of his collections at home. Mr. Tomassetti rises in all his charnel glory from behind the chopping block, lays down a bouquet of ribs, perhaps. The bow of his apron ties off his rump where a man's back should start above the buttocks.

"How many you want?" the butcher says to a housewife, "how many pork chops you want? These will go nice in a big pot of sauce. That's prime pork, Mrs. Spinelli."

"Here, boy, have some chips and run along, I got work," he might say to Lewis when his customer, another parishioner, has left. "Give my respects to your father." He would move, maybe, toward the coldroom door, open it, and disappear into its intoxicating coolness.

At last it is time. Lewis drags his feet through the suffocating heat back toward Agostino's candy store. While he has been walking Lewis has been thinking about many things: What will it be like when he has gotten to high school finally? What will he turn into at last, a moth or a butterfly? But mostly about the lemon ice. His lips have puckered and his mouth has tried to water, but his throat is a column of aching parchment.

While he has been waiting, has it gotten cooler? It is almost as though he is inhabiting two different days at the same time, for yes — he has felt the breath of autumn stirring and rustling among the leaves. He has felt the roughness of gooseflesh upon his arms, and he has shivered. Now, crossing the avenue, jaywalking past the church, he looks down at the pavement and feels as though his eyes are farther from it, as though there is a further distance between him and the earth. It is as though there were a piece of glass between his vision and the envisioned, a sheet of glass not quite clear, slightly tinted, so subtly colored that he could almost, but not quite, swear there is nothing there at all. He stops to kneel, to bend and tie his shoe — it does not truly need tying, but he wants to see if the distance he is experiencing is physical.

It is not. Nothing changes, although he can feel the movement of change all about him. He shakes his head as though to clear it, rises, and walks on. He comes to the door of the shop and goes in, and then he feels it strongly.

He looks at Mrs. Agostino and notices for the first time what she is wearing — it is a long black dress made of some sort of semi-shiny material, not the usual house dress and apron. On her head there is a close-fitting hat with a black veil falling from it. There is lace trimming here and there about her person — it reminds Lewis of webs.

He looks at Mrs. Agostino, but he cannot tell whether she is returning his gaze. "One lemon ice, please," he says, holding out his money.

The old woman shakes her head. "We no got," she says, "no got no more. You want some candy, maybe?" She begins to go to the counter, but Lewis shakes his head, an enormous sorrow settling into the pit of his stomach to reside with the hunger and thirst already there. Lewis glances back at the window whose thin film of dust is a deeper tint of the glass he had imagined while he was crossing the street. Now he knows why Mrs. Agostino's veils and laces remind him of webs, for there are webs in the corners of the store, and the floor is littered with scraps of paper, even an empty pop bottle or two.

Lewis looks at the chair behind the counter where Mr. Agostino always sat tending or guarding the machine, but the seat is empty.

The flat cushion is faded and threadbare. The machine itself is empty, the gears rusty, the wood dry and stained. Lewis knows, but does not understand how he knows, that Mr. Agostino is gone for good. How can that be? He had been in the store barely a half-hour earlier.

Mrs. Agostino shuffles back to her own stool by the window, sits down, and turns her head as though to look into the street. She says nothing more. Lewis sees her hand in her lap lying palm up, the tips of the fingers trembling slightly, every now and again the whole hand giving a fitful jerk. The old lady is more stooped than ever, Lewis thinks. He stands until he begins to feel embarrassed, and then he turns to the door, opens it — the bell makes no sound beyond a small clunk as the door hits it. Lewis looks at it to see what is the matter. It has no tongue.

Outdoors it is autumn. The church and parsonage look the same, but Lewis can feel the difference — no one he knows is inside. The aquaria with his tropical fish in them no longer line the shelves before the windows of the sunporch. The guppies and betas have risen through the glass lids and swum away into thin air. His father writes his sermons no longer in the study where the green-shaded brass lamp stood on his desk throwing a yellow light upon the words about God, words that have long since browned into umber. Who knows where his mother has gone, where his brother is now?

It is autumn. Behind him the candy store stands with its door locked, the window papered over. Cotrona's market is closed, too, and so is Galuzzo's which had used to be...hadn't it turned into?..a pizza palace. Lewis's mouth is as dry as the last leaf in a book of leaves. Who knows where he is now? Perhaps it is no longer even autumn.

MOM MAY

My mother was always collecting pieces of junk and gimcracks. One of the earliest items in her hoard that I can recall was a bird in a raffia cage that jiggled and twittered when one wound it up. "Remember this?" she asked one day when I visited her on one of my leaves from the Navy. She went to a cupboard, opened the door, and pointed to the top shelf. "Can you get it down for me?"

I got a stool and handed her down the raffia cage. "Be careful now, it's very old." She took it and we both went to the table where she sat down and wound it up. It was an old toy; a yellow canary made of tin and cotton and feathers, with a bright orange beak, sat in the center of the cage. The base was tin, like a music box. A big wire key thrust out of its side. As she wound it the perch jerked and the bird went back and forth as it made several attempts to get started. When she had finished winding she put it on the table, and the bird began to bob and nod as its ratchet voice chirped out of springs and cogs.

After high school, while I was out sailing around the world on an aircraft carrier, my mother had begun signing her letters to me, "Mom May." It was an annoying pun, of a piece with her enjoying the music of Lawrence Welk and Liberace, collecting her gewgaws, and automatically bursting into tears if she couldn't get her way. My wife Jean early in our marriage discovered that tears turned me away from, not toward her, and I have seldom since seen her weep. When she does so now, I understand that something serious has occurred, but it took many years for me to overcome the aversion training mother inflicted upon her family.

Mother hadn't always been like that. Father had brought up the children of his sister, Vita Sardella, and they had a good deal of respect for their uncle's bride, "The Great Dane" as they called her when she came briefly to live with them, until I was born. But for five more years the two families continued to live in the same Buffalo, New York, neighborhood until, in 1939, we moved to Meriden, Connecticut, leaving my aunt and cousins behind. In particular my girl cousins, "Little" Josie ("Big" Josie was married to my cousin Joseph) and Sarah, tell stories of how, when they couldn't turn to their own old-country mother for information about such things as menstrual problems, my mother would show them how modern American women had learned to cope. The cousins would always be grateful for mother's expertise in such matters and for her willingness to discuss them.

I did not know this woman myself. By the time I was old enough to begin forming coherent memories, mother was on her way to becoming a second-class citizen in the world and in the family. Father was partly to blame, for he was well into middle-age when he married and too set in the old-country attitudes toward women to change much. He wasn't cruel — there was never a less cruel man; he was just too wrapped up in his ministerial vocation to take notice of her. That was too much to bear for a woman who had hauled herself out of nineteenth-century, midwestern rural poverty by a sheer act of sustained willpower triggered by, evidently, a religious experience of some sort. It was also an insult to a trained missionary who felt she too had a calling to be something other than a parent.

She was thirty-five when I was born, set in her ways herself, independent, better educated than her husband, much more practical. When my father informed her — having himself led the life of a Lothario before he got religion and stopped sowing wild oats — that sex had only one purpose, procreation, and then followed that edict up with non-action, her sense of her worth must have plummeted into the pool of self-pity that she renewed with tears of frustration for most of the rest of her life. But of course I understood none of this until it was far too late to do anything, even if something could have been done.

Nevertheless, Mom May had always wanted to serve people. All she asked in return were continuing expressions and postures of gratitude. She wished to be surrounded by adoring crowds of Italian folk for whom she was willing to make great sacrifices, provided only that they understood her superior position. I don't believe she ever realized that everyone, including her two sons, could sense her essentially condescending nature, despite the good she certainly did for people.

Father, on the other hand, was willing to give his time, his strength, and even his limited money to the impoverished, the helpless, the troubled, and he did so without so much as a hint of anything but kindness and charity. As a result, everyone loved father, whose greatest failing was that he assumed everyone else saw things exactly as he did and was willing to do as much.

Almost no one liked mother, who was infuriated by the street people my father brought home from time to time to share our frugal Depression meals. Little Josie has told me that she and her siblings often went hungry, when father was living with them, because of this habit of her uncle. It seemed to them that it was always their rations and their mother's, not his, that were cut in order to make the meals stretch to cover the unwelcome strangers.

The first incident involving mother that I remember hearing about, and the one that set the tone of our entire life in Meriden, had to do with Miss Delphine Avery, the unmarried missionary lady who was attached to the First Italian Baptist Church, which father was selected to lead in 1939. Miss Avery, though she too was a Yankee, was well-liked by the church people. The tale as I heard it was that the congregation was not large enough to contain two trained missionaries, one of whom was the minister's wife. It was alleged that when father defended Miss Avery against Mom May's encroachments, he was accused of disloyalty and mother began to imagine that there was something going on between Papa and Miss Avery — there was assuredly nothing going on between Mom May and Papa, not until they agreed to give me a brother five years younger than I.

The folklore of the church holds that mother's forays against Miss Avery grew in bitterness and frequency, and eventually Miss Avery decided that she could do work elsewhere with more effect and less stress. Mom May stood triumphant — the parishioners maintain — among the wreckage of whatever career she had hoped to have in that church, and there are church people who still remember angrily, or so they believe, what mother did, though it is decades since father led the little flock of immigrants and a few other strayed sheep that he had managed to round up on the streets of the city.

It is a measurement of the degree to which the parish folk disliked my mother that this construction of events involving Miss Avery is completely false, according to the missionary herself. It is at this point that a series of coincidences begins: When I was a child, my father was a counselor for a year or two at Royal Ambassadors Boy's Camp at Ocean Park in Maine — I was a camper there myself. Ocean Park was, and it still is, an interdenominational summer enclave, with a weighting toward the Baptists, on the Maine coast near Saco, a mile below Old Orchard Beach. It is also the site of one of the oldest writers' conferences in the country, the State of Maine, co-founded by Adelbert Jakeman and my dear late friend, Loring Williams, who was largely responsible for the publication of my *First Poems* in 1960, and wholly responsible for the publication of my chapbook *The Sketches* two years later.

Another feature of Ocean Park is a retirement village for religious workers. When I was serving as poet-in-residence at the writers' conference during the summer of 1988, I was handed a message that Delphine Avery had been in the audience for one of my programs and wanted to say hello. It was too late for us to get together that summer, but I phoned her, and the next year Jean and I took her out to lunch where we got the true story from her.

Miss Avery said that missionaries are sent out to a place for a maximum period of two years, and after that they are automatically reassigned, because the Italian Baptist Association doesn't want any parish to grow too dependent on them. The missionary's job is to get things organized and running, and then to hand over the reins to the preacher. Unfortunately, my father came a year late to Meriden, so Delphine had stayed that extra year, and bonds that were perhaps too strong had developed between her and some of the parishioners — Delphine told us that day that some of the Meriden people still come to Ocean Park to visit her once or twice a year. She professed to know nothing of any problem between herself and Mom May. We had to believe her, and I'm grateful I had a chance to learn the true tale from one of the principals, but I now know more than I want to about the rumor-mongering that goes on in a Christian congregation.

Although mother wasn't tall, she was somewhat taller than papa who was about five-foot-five, I would surmise. She gave the impression that she was tall, though, because she was square-shouldered, she had good posture — which no doubt she had been taught in school, and she was sturdily built. People think that my own coloring — dark brown hair, brown eyes, ruddy complexion — must be ethnic, inherited from my father, but in fact that was my mother's coloring, for papa had jet black hair, gray eyes, and skin so fair that he and a similarly-colored sister (not Vita) were called the "Prince" and "Princess" in Riesi, Sicily, when they were children.

Mother could do many things with her hands when she was called upon to do so, things like bookbinding and making costumes, that she had been taught in missionary school and were supposed to be put to use in Sunday school. Gradually, though, over the years, as she made more — and more intransigent — enemies, these skills grew rusty and finally deteriorated into mere file-keeping and album-arranging. Yet wherever we moved we carried with us relics and mementos of her past projects.

I would love to go up into the attic of whatever house we were living in at the time and poke around in the trunks. There I would find things like old suits of mail — made of silver-painted burlap left over from a church pageant Mom May had staged in some archaic year before history had begun with my birth. One Halloween when I was five or six years old, she let me wear Sir Galahad's costume, complete with cardboard shield and wooden sword, and I won a five dollar prize for it at the city contest in Columbus Park. When I was older and mother had lost interest in the old costumes, my friend Dicky Hass and I dueled with those swords in the driveway of the parsonage, the battles stopping only when the weapons fell apart or our thumbs got mashed.

As time windled along, Mom May was reduced among our parishioners and our neighbors — which included much of the town one way and another, for we moved nearly every year until the church purchased a parsonage — to the status of resident curmudgeon. When I was very young I recall vividly a handyman named Mr. Scully, when he had been called upon to erect a clothes pole at our house on Newton Street and had spent a long while listening to Mom May's blistering directions and criticisms, turning to me and saying, "I would do anything for your father, but for your mother...nothing!"

At last she had left only a single bosom friend, a nasty-tempered farm woman whom Gene and I called "Clara Cow." We would come home and find Clara sitting, with her rangy frame and broad, scowling face, in the living room drinking coffee and chatting with mother in a whiny, drawly voice. I recall Clara best in the house on South Avenue that my parents managed to buy from their landlady's sister — oddly enough, they had gotten along very well with their last landlady, and Mom May was genuinely sorry when she died. The sister, knowing they had been friends, sold mama and papa the house at an extremely reasonable price. These were the early years of my marriage, when Jean and I were living in Storrs, Connecticut, Iowa City, and Cleveland.

But it was in the earlier dwellings of my childhood that I really saw most of Clara, who had never been married. Although she lived on a farm, her father, as I recall, had been a judge. For some reason, Clara would take every opportunity to insult or belittle me, even when I was a child, and I assume she did the same to my brother Gene. When I was an adult, Clara would ask me about my first teaching job at Fenn College in Cleveland, and then point out how much more money her father made as a judge, and what a superior social position he occupied. I eventually got over being annoyed or angry with Clara and simply ignored her. At last even this final friendship dissolved, and my mother was left to fight with the neighbors.

For she had even alienated her younger son and his wife who, during the first years of their marriage, lived on the first floor of the South Avenue house, which the landlady had once occupied. Gene had gone into the Navy a year after I was discharged, and when he had completed his hitch he got a job and married — he had never been interested in going to college. While he and his family lived with our parents, after work and on weekends he labored to put the somewhat run-down and old-fashioned place into excellent order. For one thing, he tore out and dug up the dirt cellar and poured a concrete floor all by himself.

When Gene and Judi's first child, Stephen, was born, papa was overjoyed. He loved being able to play with and take care of the baby, but Mom May liked to order Judi around and tell her how badly she was raising her child. At last Judi made Gene buy their own home in

Bristol, about twenty miles from Meriden, where Judi's family lived, and they moved out. The rift that existed between Judi and Mom May was never to be bridged.

After papa died Mom May participated in senior citizen activities. She took bus trips here and there, and she even went to Hawaii where she bought a small round plastic pseudo-aquarium with plastic fish swimming in it, but she eventually lost interest even in going to the various Meriden churches — any of them but my father's old place, by then known as the Grace Baptist and under the direction of a young non-Italian preacher. She was left to sit alone then in her living room looking out the windows at the neighbors who were always trying to get away with something. She had her gewgaws about her, and extras stashed in the closets and the attic to give away to anyone who might happen along and stumble into her dusty web. She had her Liberace records and the television set papa had been watching the night he pitched forward into death.

One day I drove down to Meriden from Oswego, New York, to visit and take Mom May to a reading of my poetry that I had been invited to present in New York City. I had used to stay in an attic room at the South Avenue place — actually, a finished room in the unfinished third floor of the house — but mother wanted me to sleep on a couch in the living room because she'd not "had the time" to clean upstairs. She'd also not had the time to clean downstairs, or to buy food for herself, let alone me, to eat. I took her out for dinner.

In the middle of the night the antique couch collapsed and I awoke in distress and confusion, choking in an explosion of dust bunnies. The next morning I found there was not even coffee in the house for breakfast.

Mom May enjoyed New York at noon of a bright, sunny day, where I read in Battery Park among a listless smore of noon lunchers and a few poets and friends. On my way back to Oswego I stopped at

Gene's and told him mother could no longer take care of herself. Though he had been visiting her regularly, he hadn't noticed that she became disoriented and sometimes didn't know where she was after getting out of a car in front of her own home, was not eating right if at all, never changed or washed her clothes, didn't clean the house. It had all happened too gradually, I guess, but when I pointed out the facts, he recognized their reality.

The last time we all — both families — took Mom May out, we went for a walk in Hubbard Park in Meriden. But it was the year when the spruce budworms were devouring New England, and they hung from the park trees on their long filaments, crawled over the skeletal leaves of the trees and dropped excrement on our heads, or fell themselves down our collars. We walked on their bodies. We went shopping, then to lunch. Mother wore a men's crew-neck T-shirt under her blouse, and it was yellow. It was difficult to sit next to her, breathe normally, and eat at the same time.

Gene made arrangements, with my consent, to put Mom May into a retirement home near him just outside Bristol, and there she stayed for several years, fading into silence, paying little attention to what went on around her. She broke her hip and would no longer get out of bed. And one day, when she had long-since forgotten how to cry and no longer cared for anything at all that went on in the world, she died.

We buried her next to the ashes of our father in Walnut Grove Cemetery in Meriden. We were solemn, but there were no tears except for those of Jean's and my high-school friend, Marie. She had recently lost her own widowed mother, with whom she had lived in her childhood home for several years after divorce, and of whom she had complained most of her life. Now, she found that she could weep for us all. "It's so much harder than I thought it would be," she said.

When I think back I remember Mom May best in the summertime, on an evening heavy with heat that wrapped the parsonage on Windsor Avenue in its smothering arms. As I stare out of the window of the bedroom I share with my brother Gene, a crisp breeze comes walking down the row of thick elms that stop abruptly at the corner where the Italian neighborhood starts. The breeze seems like a breath of September. It is cool. It clears my nostrils and smells fresh. It darkens my blues. Fall has always been a melancholy season, I recall, but fall in June is nearly unbearable. I rise to go downstairs.

My father, like some scuttler of the deep, has retreated from the family eye into his study in the sunporch.

Mother is in the kitchen. I walk past her, out the screen door, letting it slam behind me on its spring. "Where are you going?" she asks. "It's late to be going out, isn't it?"

I look at her through the dusty mesh — she is perspiring and dabbing her face with a soggy handkerchief. She is sitting at the table. A plate of what had been ice-cream is at her elbow. She faces away from it toward me. Her hair is still solid brown, though she is well into middle age, and she looks as oaken as the trees her father had felled to build the Wisconsin farmstead which, once sown, had sprung to seed at once.

"I'll be back in a while. It's hot. It ought to be nice driving." I start down the back steps. "Want to come?"

She shakes her head. I leave her and the clock humming above the range to revolve the summer slowly in silence. I go out to the smashed pear tree dying beside the house; my '40 Chevy jalopy is parked under its wickety limbs, and I get in, start it. I back out of the drive.

Soon I am clattering along the roads at the western edge of town. The furtive moon rearrives and shines through the windshield; the clouds lift and there are stars. The hills around town pull me in and I drive up through Hubbard Park to Castle Craig, a tower some rich man long ago had built on East Peak, the little crop of rocks no large state would dare to call mountains. Castle Craig belongs to the city now, and

I mount its black throat to come out again into the night. I look down on the place where I've grown up.

The night is cool, the breeze is edgy and surreptitious among the leaves of the woods below. I stand and watch the lights out there, downward past Mirror Lake reservoir. And as I look, seeing the ripples of darkness glimmer and fade in the water and in the streets and yards of Meriden, it seems as though my blues have been dipped into the basin of understanding and come out pure. I know, for this brief space of clear time, the difference between sadness and guilt, between self-pity and scorn.

The Italian Baptist Church boys, 1944, Lewis Turco in the center

GENE AND GENES

Now and then father's sister, Aunty Vita Sardella, would come down for a visit from Buffalo where I had been born and father had begun his clerical career. She would always bring some of our cousins, Joseph and Salvatore, Josephine and Sarah — the young women had baby-sat me when I was a toddler, but Sal was my favorite. They were all protestants too, but not converted in this country — the Turcos had been Waldensians in Riesi, Sicily, where there had been a Waldensian church since the middle ages. Gene, who was five years younger than I and had never lived in Buffalo, was more or less a stranger to the Sardella family.

Mother was May Laura Putnam, part English and part Danish, so Gene and I are a mixed breed both ethnically and religiously. When I was five years of age, my brother was born in Meriden. His middle name is "Laurent"— the female version of "Laura," my mother's middle name; it was many years before I realized the derivation of "Gene": it is the American version of "Gino," which is short for "Luigi"— my father had named both his sons after himself!

It was not until we were seven and twelve years of age respectively that Gene and I learned about mother's people. During the summer of 1946 mother took us on our first and only trip to visit her family in the Middle West, where she had been raised. "Mom May," as she took to signing her letters toward the end of her life, had been born in Wayne, Nebraska, on May Day, 1899, the third of nine children — including six sons and three daughters — in the family of William Herbert

Putnam, eighty-nine that year; his second wife, Laura Christina Larsen Putnam, was seventy-two, the mother — so far as we know — of all his children. The family had moved to Superior, Wisconsin, during mother's childhood, and all her family were still living in that area with the exception of her sister Lillian, who had died young.

I was old enough to have begun to understand that our family was very poor. When father died I saw some of his old tax records and documents, and as a Baptist preacher he had never made more than $2500.00 a year in his life. Still, my brother and I were raised as though we were members of the middle class, and our expectations were middle class expectations — there is a great deal to be said, it seems to me, for the way in which people think of themselves, as distinguished from their actual financial situation. When we got to Superior I saw what real poverty was all about.

The Putnam homestead was a large oblong shack of two storeys standing near a barn which, it seems to me looking back over this cairn of years, was in better shape than the house whose weathered clapboards showed no sign of having been painted during modern times. Indoors, the floor undulated in great waves of worn wood. I don't believe there was a cellar underneath the building. Certainly there was no insulation, for there were no plaster walls. The only thing between the inner and outer climates was the sheathing of pine. In fact, it was nothing more than a barn itself.

The house was heated by a large free-standing wood stove in the middle room, and by a wood-burning cast iron cookstove in the kitchen where the zinc sink had no faucets, only a hand pump. There was no other indoor plumbing. Instead, Gene and I were introduced for the first time in our lives to privy facilities. I for one was glad we were visiting in midsummer rather than winter, though the yellow jackets and wasps that called the out-house home were something of a concern.

In the house an unenclosed stairway rose to the second floor where the bedrooms were located. We must have stayed in one or two of them, but I have no recollection of having done so. I do remember finding a large stone filled with amethysts on the stairs. I admired it so much that Grandma gave it to me, and I brought it back to Meriden where I added it to the bookcase museum I had in the bedroom Gene and I shared in the parsonage.

I have but one clear memory of Grandpa, a lean old man with a stubble beard who didn't bother with the privy for certain necessities if it weren't convenient. I had gone out into the yard and was wandering about the place when I caught him standing up against the outside wall of the barn relieving himself, giving the sere planks a good soaking. When he caught sight of me he buttoned himself up and disappeared like smoke into a breeze. I seldom spotted him after that, and always only at a distance.

Grandma was much more in evidence during our visit. I have no recollection of hearing her speak, though she must have done so, of course. She was a pure second-generation Danish-American, born in Manistee, Michigan, of parents who had immigrated from Denmark. It is this fact that led my Sicilian relatives in Buffalo to refer to my mother as "The great Dane." There was both affection and disdain in that pun.

Grandma's demeanor was always grim. She had no sense of humor, so far as I could tell — no more than mother had. She always wore an apron, whether in or out of the house; she was always busy cooking or cleaning or darning socks and had little time for a prepubescent grandson. Still, for some reason I fell in love with her and I liked to go with her when she had to attend to errands or chores.

Despite the fact that the homestead was called a "farm," it had no land other than that on which the buildings stood, so Grandma's garden plot was located in a vacant lot several blocks away. Each day when she went to gather raspberries or vegetables I went with her to help and to carry some of the things back to the house. On the way we stopped at least once at a corner store where they sold ice cream cones dipped to order in various candy sprinkles. I can taste the colors still.

Our uncles were all very large men, generally affable and easy-going. None of them still lived on the homestead. Gene and I had two favorites — Uncle Arny and, our absolute favorite, Uncle Ed, who worked in a steel mill and stood well over six feet tall. We still own a snapshot of him with Gene, me, and his two sons draped all over him as he stands grinning into the camera. Family legend has it that a young man at the steel mill once decided that he wanted to make his mark and chose to try to pick a fight with the biggest man around, Ed Putnam. Uncle Ed ignored him or brushed off his sallies and insults for a time, which only infuriated the young man more. At last he took a swing at Ed who didn't bother to swing back, but merely caught the approaching fist in his own hand and began to squeeze and bend the young fellow's wrist back. When at last the attacker was kneeling on the floor at Uncle Ed's feet, gritting his teeth in pain, Ed suggested that an apology was in order and a cessation of hostilities. He got both and there was no more trouble between them.

When we visited the farm of Uncle Arthur Bakken — who had married Aunt Myrtle, four years older than mother — he took Gene and me fishing at a lake nearby. Gene caught eight fish off one side of the boat, and I caught three off the other. When I insisted on trading sides, Gene caught five more, but I caught only four. On another occasion all the men and boys were bringing in hay on a flat-bed, open-slat, horse-drawn wagon. I was allowed to drive the wagon and was doing a good and prideful job of it when I stepped slightly to one side. My leg slipped down between the slats, which were covered with a thin layer of hay, and I was caught solid, held by the boards clear up to my crotch. I had the most enormous, purple-yellow bruise the full length of my thigh, but the thing that hurt worst was my failure as a driver. Clearly, life had it in for me.

Of the brothers only Harvey, born in 1897, was older than mother. Arnold was next in line, born in 1900, and Ed was third youngest, born in 1906. Of them all, May was the only one who managed to pull herself away from Wisconsin-Minnesota and attend college. She went to Chicago where she enrolled in secretarial school and became a stenographer during the heyday of the famous mobsters. She told us that one of them was gunned down on the street where she lived, almost beneath her window.

Where and when she got religion I do not know, but it was her ambition to become a missionary. She migrated east and managed, working as a secretary, to put herself through the School of Religious Education of Boston University where she took her bachelor's degree. Afterward she began to do work among the Italian immigrants near Wakefield, Massachusetts, and it was there that she met father, who had converted to Protestantism and started on the road to becoming a minister.

One of Mom May's legacies to me were two albums filled with pictures, documents, letters, and memorabilia of various kinds, all of these arranged in chronological order. The most interesting item in them, to me, is this letter written on letterhead of the Colgate-Rochester Divinity School and datelined "December 19, 1932":

> Dear Miss Putnam,
>
> I know that you do not welcome my correspondence, but that does not matter. I do not like to reciprocate the same attitude, or in other words: I do not want to act according to the Old Testament procedure, namely, eye for eye, tooth for tooth. I like to think of you, gently, of those beautiful days of Christian friendship which we spent

together in that Methodist Camp, and once [a] year, at least, I want to share it to you by sending to you a Christmas card.

This year is a special Christmas for me, therefore, I am accompanying my Christmas card with this letter. The speciality consists that the second Sunday of December I began a new work in Buffalo. At the corner of Rhode Island and Normal Ave. there is a beautiful American church. It is a modern building of bricks, and it [is] surrounded by 40,000 Italians. All the American people have almost moved elsewhere, and the Buffalo Baptist Union decided to begin our Italian mission. The English meetings still continue, but in addition to them I began the work in Italian. The American minister is still there, of course, who carries the work in English. The time will come when that church will fall completely in the hands of the Italians. Then I shall be happy to be at the head of two big churches. In the morning now I am preaching in my old church, the Second Italian Baptist Church, in which I enjoy to preach to a congregation of more than one hundred individuals, in the afternoon I preach in this new church; last Sunday I had 17 persons. It is very good at the beginning. I feel now that God has called me to do an outstanding piece of work here in Buffalo where we have a colony of 75,000 Italians.

As far as school is concerned this is my last year of my theological course; I need only 28 hours of credit to finish my college work. It is almost another year of work then I shall be glad to be thru [sic] and receive my two degrees. This will give me a great confidence and courage in thinking that my education is not inferior to certain Italian and

American pastors who look down at the poor missionaries who have not a college and seminary education.

You may question now to yourself, "Why is Mr. Turco telling to me that?" The answer will be this: because my heart is full of joy and I need some one to manifest this joy, and I selected you, this time, to be the recipient to pour the joy of my heart. Do you not appreciate it?

Cordially yours,
L. Turco

When our parents were married the following year, mother was already thirty-four years of age and father was forty-three. I have believed for years that they ought not to have gotten together. It was a disaster for her, for it brought to an end the long process of her turning herself into something extraordinary. Not that father was in any way unkind — I can hardly imagine a more compassionate man, but his upbringing in the old country had been typical. He was the man of the house, it was his calling that came first, and mother necessarily came second. It was more than she could bear, and she died a very unhappy and unfulfilled woman.

Life, however, is full of paradoxes. Mother and father had found it necessary to take industrial jobs during the second world war. Afterward mother kept working, though as a stenographer, not a production-line worker, and father became the homemaker and housekeeper, because his vocation kept him around the house most of the time.

When Mom May came to Massachusetts from Chicago she was returning to her roots, for she was a direct descendant of Constable "Carolina" John Putnam who, in 1692, was rounding up the innocent citizens of Salem Village and dragging them off to jail to await trial for witchcraft. According to the family genealogy, *The Putnam Lineage* by Eben Putnam, published in Salem when Mom May was eight years old, the Putnam family, in the persons of John Putnam, his wife and sons, had settled in Salem by 1639 or 1640.

Furthermore, according to Eben Putnam, George Puttenham, purported author of *The Arte of English Poesy* (1589), was a member of the clan in a line that had become extinct. Curiously, I had not known about this until several years after I had published my own *The Book of Forms: A Handbook of Poetics* in 1968, but I had been aware of the family link with the Salem trials in a vague way as early as high school. Some of my first writing was on the subject, for during my junior year at Meriden High I wrote a "Witch Trial" script for Senior Skit Night in 1951. Our club, The Fantaseers, performed it to vast local acclaim.

The year before, I had written in Doc Michel's sophomore English class an addendum — a final chapter imitating Nathaniel Hawthorne's style — to *The House of the Seven Gables*. I kept wondering about Salem, however, so in middle age I researched and wrote a 1200-page manuscript, *The Devil's Disease, A Narrative of the Age of Witchcraft in England and New England 1580-1697*. It is still unpublished, but I now know more than I really wanted to about the Putnams of America, nearly all of whom are descended from one immigrant Buckinghamshire family.

When she was younger, my mother wrote also. I have found copies of some of her religiously-oriented stories in the meticulous secretarial files she kept on everyone throughout her life. In those same files I have found many of my own early attempts to write, most of them stories of science fiction or the supernatural. To judge from these facts one might surmise that there are two genetic traits that have continued down through the years of the lineage: first, a strong religious streak that takes some strange twists and, second, an equally strong literary bent that arises among the Putnams from time to time despite the environment, for there are many members of the family who are publishers, librarians, and writers including my daughter, Melora, who is a librarian. An even greater number, however, are artisans, laborers, soldiers and farmers. My brother Gene is a toolmaker, and I am a writer. It's a curious heritage.

My mother was the only one of the Putnam siblings to exhibit the literary and religious traits both, and she passed them on to me, except that in my case the religious bent was bent backwards. I continue to write fantasies, although I have spent years trying to break myself of the habit, but fortunately "magical realism" is currently a popular and respectable type of fiction. However, I lost my religion — if ever I had it truly — about the same time as our trip to Wisconsin.

Mother took Gene and me to a beach on one of Wisconsin's many beautiful lakes. I recall another child's body flung up on the sand, its flesh blue, a pallid blue. Gene had seen the child also, as he has told me in recent years. Though I've thought of the accident often over the decades, I didn't discuss it with anyone until after mother's death, not even Gene.

One day after we had gotten back to Meriden from that trip to Wisconsin I experienced a revelation — I felt I was absolutely in this physical world where I did not particularly want to be. It was clear in that moment of enlightenment that one had to make the best of the situation, for I was certain this world is the only one there is. There was nothing for it but to try to become a writer, to invent imaginary worlds into which people might escape at times, as I was able to do when I read a good book. It would be a game. I would fill my time with seeing how far whatever talent I had could occupy my mind before I had to take my place among the shells on the beach, like Mom May, our uncles and aunts Putnam, Aunty Vita and father, for all of them are gone now, and Gene and I have taken their places, despite my warning to him many years ago not to tag along.

FATHER AND SON

My son, he thinks that I am dead, but it is not true. How can a man be dead if he has sons? He is a good son. I wished that he would be a minister, to follow in the footsteps of his father and to serve God, but it could not be so, and he is a poet instead.

To be a poet is a great honor in my home country, Sicily, so my son honors his father. I wished always to be able to speak the English well, and to write it, but I could not master it. It may be that I can do it better by speaking through my son — I must do it anyway, because my body is ashes, and ashes have not a tongue.

Before I became ashes I wrote a book about my life, and I asked my son to read it and to make the English of it correct. He did not do it at that time. Now he is working on my book — it is a penance; it is his way to put my ashes on his head, as the old monks used to do it. I forgive him, I never blamed him. It is the way of the flesh.

He could not believe in my religion, and it made my heart ache, but as he reads my book, he is discovering that we were closer than he thought. The poet is a religious man too who wishes to know the power that is within and the power that is without. My son believes, but he is afraid to believe, for if he is wrong it will destroy him. This is what he thinks.

I became what men call "dead" on Wednesday, September 18, 1968. On Sunday, the 15th, my son had a premonition, and so he called me from the New York State to Connecticut to ask me not to shovel the snow in the winter. I promised I would not shovel it, but I did not like my medicine for *high blood pressure, and so I did not take it. My son cannot forgive himself that he did not find out that I did this, and he does not forgive me.*

Now that he has edited my book, my son is writing a memoir for an introduction. I hope it will have not too much sentiment.

The first poem I wrote about Luigi, my father, was titled "An Immigrant Ballad." When it was published in my *First Poems* in 1960 and my mother read it, she took me to task over the poem. How could I say such things, and put them in a book? My father, who had been in the next room and had overheard the argument, came into the kitchen where we were talking and interrupted us. "But it is true!" he said, "it is all true!" The argument must have continued for a while, but that's all of it I remember, because for me it ended with my father's remark, which was typical of him — if a thing were true, it was true, and peace! He believed in the truth, and he tried to live it. No man I ever met tried harder.

I was surprised to discover later, from my cousin, "Little" Josephine, how true the poem in fact was. I had taken what I thought were some poetic liberties — for instance, my father's mandolin playing — but, according to Josie, he had, indeed, played the mandolin in his youth. I had never seen or heard any such thing in our house during the years my brother Gene and I were growing up. Why? Because we were products of his second lifetime, for my father had lived two utterly different lives, one when he was a young hedonist, a second after his spiritual rebirth.

My father speaks, in the first of his writings I have collected in the volume on which I am working, of that rebirth and second life; he refers only obliquely to the first life, as he did prior to his sudden death by heart failure or stroke. What I know of his youth is fragmentary, and it owns the quality of legend. Family talk with my cousins — all of whom are older than I, some of them considerably (two of them deceased early, including one I never met) — who grew up with their uncle as I was to do later, has provided me with some information, but not much. I got even less from my father, who now and then told anecdotes out of the past, but they were few and usually humorous. He lived in the present, and for the future. The past was merely trial, a preliminary to his rebirth, which took place when he was already a man.

One of the stories he sometimes told was of a young man in Sicily who wanted to be Someone, with a capital S. The way to be Someone was to join the Mafia. Somewhere the boy who was to be my sire made contact with a Mafia member who said he could get him into the organization. They made an appointment to meet, and my father went home. Before the appointment he managed to get hold of a pistol. When the time came, he stuck the gun in his belt, feeling like a Big Shot, and set out to meet his contact.

As he was swaggering down the street he heard a commotion ahead of him. He came down to earth in time to notice a cordon of carabinieri coming up the road — they were conducting a house-to-house search for someone. My father, with a very guilty conscience, assumed they were looking for him — somehow they had heard of his appointment to join the Mafia! He jammed the revolver under his shirt, slunk back to his house, and hid, trembling, under the bed.

At last he heard the carabinieri stop outside the door. Through the open window he heard one of them ask, "Whose house is this?" Another answered, "Oh, that's Signor Turco's house. He's a respectable citizen. Leave it alone," and they passed on by.

Under the bed the boy lay, feeling sick and greatly relieved. My grandfather's reputation had saved him — it was, no doubt, a Sign. He got rid of the pistol and never kept the appointment. There were other ways to be Somebody, and he would find one of them. Meanwhile, he would be alive and out of jail.

To hear and watch my father tell this story was to witness a polished comic performance. It was hilarious to see him imitating himself as a Big Shot, the gun stuck in his pants, rolling along the road among the pigs and chickens until the sight of the law froze him in Chaplinesque horror. I wouldn't want anyone to think he was some dour Calvinist or pompous Parson Goodbody.

I understand "Calvinist," but I do not understand "Goodbody." I think it may be too sentimental. I was not a Puritan, but my wife was. She was not an Italian, and that is why, I think, I did not speak so much about my youth in Italy. My wife wanted our two sons to be Americans, and she did not understand my background. She is from Wisconsin, a Methodist missionary who worked with the Italian immigrants. I met her in a camp in Wakefield, Massachusetts, where we both were working with the immigrants, and I was going to be a Protestant minister.

People think it is strange for an Italian to be a minister, but in Sicily is the home of the Waldensians, a very old sect of Protestants, even much older than the Puritans. A Waldensian church is in my native village of Riesi.

But it was not the Waldensians who converted me, it was in this country, the Episcopalians. The men of Sicily are not very religious. It is the women who are religious because they have very hard lives. The men have hard lives, too, but the Roman Catholic Church supports the State, and the State has no interest in Sicily— they think we are all Africans. So the men of Sicily do not support the Church or the State. The Mafia is the government. The Mafia is the only strong power in Sicily.

In this country when I came the Roman Catholic Church was in the control of the Irish people. The Irish people did not want poor people from the south of Italy to be members of their congregations. They did not want other immigrants, either. So, when the Italians wanted to worship, the Irish gave them the church basement to use until they could build their own church, or they gave them nothing.

So it was the Protestant denominations who sent missionaries to help the immigrants, and some of us were converted. But this is a strange thing, too, for there is prejudice everywhere. It is not Christian. Though the Episcopalians converted me, they were not hospitable to Italians, and I had to become a Baptist. Many Italians became Baptists, members of the Italian Baptist Association of America, affiliated with the Northern Baptist Convention. The Italian Baptists had several churches, especially in the East, but in California there also were some.

My wife was prejudiced against Italians too, but I do not think she knew it. She wanted to do good works among them, but she never became one of them. They sensed this. So, in the home I told very little of my old life, and I did not speak the Italian language. My children were raised as Americans. But so were all of the children of the church: the second generation had little understanding of their heritage, and they did not want to know it. Their parents, too, wanted to become Americans, and if they could not do it, then they would be sure the sons and daughters could. Now, I am ashamed that my sons were raised without knowing their father's life and family.

I seem to have been trying to capture my father in words for most of my life, and perhaps he is going to elude me again this time. I remember doing a paper in the 8th or 9th grade while I was enrolled in Suffield Academy, a private, Baptist-affiliated school in Connecticut, where my father insisted I be sent to get the best education possible, as he saw it, and which he could not afford. The paper was titled something like, "My Father: My Ideal." But the piece that gets closest, I think, was an early poem titled "Luigi." It spoke of the deep humanity of his personality, of his determination to live the life a true Christian is supposed to live, not merely pay lip-service to.

I don't think my father ever realized — perhaps I didn't, either, for a long time — that one important reason I couldn't follow in the path he blazed was that he provided a model for me, and for nearly everyone else who knew him, that most people could not live up to. I saw the difference between what a Christian was supposed to be, and what most in fact were. I early understood the nature of hypocrisy. Rather than be a hypocrite myself, I eschewed conventional piety. I could never hope to be as good as my father, so I wouldn't try.

While he was alive I didn't publish his sketch in a collection, but I did after his death, including it in a reprint of the series, *The Sketches of Lewis Turco*, of which it was originally supposed to be a part. Still, the poem was not very specific, and it was his Second Life I talked about. I suppose his First Life will remain mysterious and anecdotal to me, a censored Harlequinade, the juicier parts left out. And I want the juice so that I can conjure him up again in the flesh, for what I don't know about him continues to haunt me. I want him human, not saintly, for I do not understand saintliness and never could, which is why I want to understand him. It is, I think, the central fact of my life that I wanted to be like him and could never understand how he got to be the way he was when I knew him. I could never believe, try as I might, as deeply as he believed, and finally I could not believe at all. The key is buried in his grave, beneath his epitaph:

> The good man
> is gone. Pray
> his eyes see now
> what his heart saw.

If there is a note of uncertainty in the words, it is mine, not his.

I loved to read the poetry of my oldest son, and I translated some of it into Italian. I printed some of it even in Protestant journals in Italy, and some is now in a book of Italian-American poetry both in Italy and in

America. But my son's poetry was dark, he used dark words, and they broke my heart. God is the light, and I wanted him always to see God. But he is like his mother. The women of her family, the Putnams, are like Sicilian women, and it is strange, for they have a grudge against life. I think that they do not like to be alive.

I cannot tell you what I "see" now that I am ashes, but everything is "light." There are no words. Nothing begins, and nothing ends.

The name Turco means, in Italian, "Turk"; it is not an uncommon name in Sicily. It dates, I understand, from the period of Arab rule in the 9th to 11th centuries. One of my father's anecdotes has to do with the name. During the Turco-Italian War, which took place between the autumns of 1911 and 1912, my father was in the Italian army, stationed well away from the front. One day the officer in charge of his unit assembled the men. He said that volunteers were needed to go to the front lines; those who volunteered were asked to step forward. My father was the only soldier to take two paces and stand at attention. The officer looked him over. "Your name is Turco, no?" he asked.

"Si," my father said.

"What would happen if you were in the trenches? Suppose someone called your name—'Turco'! The men might think an attack was coming and begin to run. No, no. You step back in line." He pointed to some others of the company—"You, you, you! Step forward!" They had volunteered, and again my father was spared. Another Sign?

At various points in his youth my father was a miner, a mechanic, a shoemaker, a soldier in the American army—even the chauffeur to the mayor of Rome! I hadn't even known he could drive, for he walked everywhere in Meriden and never owned a car. He mentions some of these careers in the autobiographical sketch, "A Brief Story of My Life." He was also a writer, though his English was never first rate. Still, he had to write at least one sermon a week for many years, some in Italian, some in English. He used to write letters to the local papers in Connecticut, and he wrote articles in Italian and English for *L'Aurora*, the monthly magazine of the Italian Baptist Association of America. The last of these articles, "The Joy of Living," appeared in the same issue with his obituary notice:

LUIGI TURCO

May 28, 1890 — September 18, 1968

The Rev. Luigi Turco, retired pastor of the Italian Baptist Church, now the Grace Baptist Church [of Meriden, Connecticut] died unexpectedly September 18th.

Mr. Turco was pastor of the Italian Baptist Church for 16 years, from 1938 to 1954, later becoming pastor of St. John the Baptist Church, Bronx, N.Y. He returned to Meriden following his retirement 10 years ago.

Born in Sicily May 28, 1890, he studied for a year in the Waldensian Seminary in Rome. He also studied at Rochester and Buffalo Universities and finished his divinity work at Colgate-Rochester School in 1933.

A veteran of World War I, he served in the U. S. Army.

Before coming to Meriden, Mr. Turco served for 12 years as pastor of the Second Italian Baptist Church of Buffalo, N.Y., and as Italian pastor of the Emmanuel Baptist Church in Buffalo for 5 years after founding an Italian mission in that church.

He was ordained into the ministry in April of 1939. Under his pastorate, land at the corner of Windsor and Springdale Avenues adjacent to the original church property was purchased, providing a six-room cottage as a parsonage. Six garages were acquired in the transaction. In addition, a building fund was created from donations by the men of the church.

In 1954, Mr. Turco returned to his hometown of Riesi, Sicily, for a long visit and preached in the local Waldensian Church.

Following his return to the United States in June of 1955 he assumed the pastorate of St. John the Baptist Church in the Bronx, N. Y., where he inaugurated services in Italian for the larger Italian community there.

He is survived by his wife, Mrs. May Putnam Turco; two sons, Lewis P. Turco, visiting professor at the State University, Potsdam, N. Y., and Gene L. Turco of Bristol, Connecticut; a grandson, Steven P. Turco of Bristol; a granddaughter, Melora Turco of Potsdam; a sister, Mrs. Gaetano Mililli, and two brothers, Salvatore Turco and Giuseppe Turco, all of Italy, and several nieces and nephews.

Funeral services were conducted by the Rev. Clinton Barlow at the Grace Baptist Church, 10:00 a.m., Saturday, September [22]. Burial was in Walnut Grove Cemetery, Meriden, Conn....

To Mrs. May P. Turco and her family we pray for the solace and strength that only God can give.

Yes, "The Joy of Living." I enjoyed to be alive, even when life was difficult. My son enjoys to be alive, too, as long as he does not think about it. Many people do not understand him, because he seems to be full of life and good humor, like the men of his mother's family — they were Nordic giants, always smiling. But when he is alone he looks in himself, and the words he takes for his poems paint the darkness of silence and emptiness. So they think his poetry does not fit his personality.

It is the darkness in my son that I am sad about. Still, if he had been a soldier in the trenches, I think he would have volunteered too. To volunteer is to love life so well that there is not the fear of death.

But I have been discouraged. When my congregation in Connecticut forced me to resign because they wanted a younger man, an American, and they wanted to Americanize the name of the Church, I was hurt and bitter. But I would not stop my life. I went to the Bronx in New York and lived in the church bell tower alone. My wife, May, stayed with my younger son, Gene, in Connecticut so he could graduate from the high school there where his friends were. The church in New York was dying, and the people of the Italian neighborhood were moving out. The area was becoming Black. When I tried to do missionary work among the Black people and to bring them into the church, the congregation there became prejudice, and I was forced to leave again. Then the church died.

I came back to Connecticut and began a church in the ballroom of an old hotel. My congregation was my younger son and three old Latvians, refugees that I sponsored after the Second World War against the wishes of my Italian Baptist congregation — they held that against me too. They called me a dictator, but I did not make them do it. When they refused to help the refugees, I took them myself to find them work and a place to live. It was not the church. The Latvian family and my younger son worshipped in the hotel. My wife would not come, and my older son, Lewis, was a sailor in the Navy, far away.

This was my church until fire destroyed the hotel. Again I despaired, but then God told me what to do: write. So I began to write.

Because of my father's near blindness it was extremely difficult for him to read and write, but after his retirement he devoted more and more time to these efforts. Toward the end of his life he became very ambitious in a literary way. The short autobiography was a preliminary to the longer "Letter to My Nephew," who was a Roman Catholic priest in Sicily, which he regarded as his major work and which he tried hard to publish — he even wrote The Beatles to enlist their aid.

On television he had heard something about The Beatles going to India to study with the Maharishi Mahesh Yogi. It reminded him of an episode in Buffalo when he had some sort of spiritual adventure with a yogi. Since both he and The Beatles had shared similar psychic experiences, surely they would be interested in helping to publish his religious book? He never got a reply, so far as I know. Obviously, another crank letter — the incident gave me some insight into crankhood. "Cranks" like my father, whatever else may be said of them, are true believers, at least twice as real, in all their innocence, as the electric images the rest of us live with in the "real" world. I am convinced that my father was more real than I am, and that is what makes him so ghostly.

It was when I was a shoemaker that I damaged my eye. The husband of my sister Vita left Sicily to come to the United States, and he promised her that when he took a job and saved some money, then he would send for her and his family. So Vita and her children waited. They waited for a long time, but there was no money in his few letters.

So Vita decided to start a shoe factory and to save the money herself. I asked her if I may accompany her and work with her. She said yes, so I worked. One day I was trying to pull a nail out of a shoe with pliers. The nail came out suddenly and it went into my good eye, so I was blind in that eye. The other eye was not good.

But we saved the money, and we took a ship. When we came to Massachusetts we found her husband working in a tavern and drinking. We lived in squalor. The baby was in an orange box, and a rat crawled on her. I began to tell my sister that I would save the family, that her husband would not do it, that he was not a good Christian. And so I began to study. I finished the high school, and I began to study for the ministry.

But look at the dark words of my son in his poem. I do not understand it, what he says, but it does not sound correct. The "wings" do not "fail me." The "wind" does not "blow from darkness into dark." I have no "tricks to sustain me." It is my son speaking not of me, but of himself, as he did on the epitaph that he put on my stone. He is full of doubt.

My father's story had come to haunt me by the time he was living in the house he and my mother had bought on South Avenue after years of moving from one neighborhood to another. But the house in which I remember him best was the parsonage. We moved into it when I was in junior high school, before I went to Suffield. After years of planning and saving, the church had bought it, and for a while we had some feeling of physical location, a point of reference and a neighborhood.

One of the features of the house was the enclosed sunporch of which I have written several times in these pages. For years after I had left the family for the Navy, marriage, college, I would dream of that room, the black angelfish swimming in the air. I have tried many times to write of it, in a story, and again in a poem titled "The Recurring Dream." Once I'd written the poem, I stopped having that particular dream, for I had exorcised it in the act of writing. But then I had others, and I wrote to exorcise them, too. Poetry is a true therapy, which I think my father would understand.

The parsonage was my great pride. For years the church saved to buy it. But it was only one house that we lived in, and my son does not remember much the house in Buffalo where I lived with the family of my sister Vita. I was the head of that house too. We went from Massachusetts when I became a minister, leaving the husband behind. I converted my sister and her children and took them out of the squalid surroundings. My nieces, when they grew up, did not like it that I took them away from their father, but my nephews who were older remembered what our life was like, and they continued to honor their uncle.

When I was married, my nieces called my wife "The Great Dane," because she was half Danish, but she loved them and was good to them. None of them approved of my marriage, not even my sister Vita. But my wife and I were almost too old to be married, thirty-four and forty-four years, and we wanted a family of our own. Ah, the things that people will do in the world! It was not a happy marriage, but we raised our two sons, and they are good sons. We have done our duty.

After he had written his autobiography and his "Letter," at the very end of his time, my father worked largely on translating some of my poems into Italian — not out of any literary consideration, but out of a desire to understand his offspring. This is clear from some of his letters. He thought in Italian, and in order to communicate he had first to translate his thoughts into English. The reverse was true as well — in order to understand English, he had to translate into Italian.

Perhaps that's all there is to it: the language barrier — I speak no Italian at all. Perhaps our groping to understand each other is merely a matter of words. At any rate, that is all we have now. On September 16, 1957, he wrote me the following letter. I will leave it as he wrote it, as an example of his pure style:

Dear Lewis,

Next month I will start a church in one of the rooms of Winthrop Hotel. Dr. Ervin Seale, pastor of the Church of the Truth of New York City, will come to Meriden to help me starting the church.

I had a letter from Dr. Uheler, a psychologist and cooworker with Dr. Seale, telling me to write a long letter to Dr. Seale in which he could see the progress of my ideas concerning the movement of The New Thought on which Religious Science Churches are based. Instead of a long letter I wrote to Dr. Seale a brief story of my life which, the enclosed in this letter, is a copy. There he will see far better than in a letter how I came to the knowledge of the New Thought movement, which is not new at all; It is as old as Christianity is, but the teachings of the Bible have been obscured by the numerous dogmas and creeds which churches, both Protestant and Catholic, have been formulated through the centuries.

I am sending this copy to you of the story of my life for correction of my English. My greatest trouble is my English Language. I am determined to master it as best as I can. So, please teach me as much English as you can. Correct this paper for me and when you come to Meriden show me all my mistakes of grammar, punctuation, construction, ect. Next Friday I shall go to New York and have an enterview with Dr. Seale to discus plans for the starting of the church. I shall be back late in the evening, (Sunday)

Enclosed you find also a card of congratulation from the Meriden Saving Bank which I opened thinking that it was my mail. This lead me to congratulate you, too. How? By a gift of $25.00. Let me buy the text books for you this year, so you owe me no money.

God bless you together with your sweet wife,

Your loving father....

For ten years after his passing — until the death of my father-in-law, John Houdlette, in 1978 — I was haunted by a recurrent dream which, with many other demons, I exorcised during the winter and spring of 1979 by writing a series of poems titled *Letters to the Dead*.

It is difficult to speak now, using the voice of my son. But he has come to believe some of the things that I believed at the end of my life. Still, there is the darkness that comes to him sometimes, the darkness that he sees instead of the light.

I do not think that I will speak again, but I will remain with him. Nothing is finished. Forever we are with one another, the all of us, living and the dead, the born and the unborn.

Lewis, Rev. Luigi, & Mom May
Turco, 1935

CURT

For a couple of years during The War — that is, World War Two — my family lived on a chicken farm, or in the farmhouse of a chicken farm I should say. Situated on Curtis Street at the edge of Meriden, the farm belonged to a man named Muenchow. His main business was a dairy farm situated not far away, and that was where he lived. The chickens were in large three-storied buildings behind the barn, which was back of the house we rented.

Curtis Street was a long road with a big bend that started at Broad Street near the Wallingford line and moved through nearly-country neighborhoods until it climbed a hill at the top of which began a more heavily populated area. The road settled there into a straight line that took it back into Broad Street on a slant where "uptown" began at the junction of Broad and East Main.

The chicken farm was at the bottom of the hill, just before country quite abruptly became town. On the crown lived my friend Jackie Tierney, a bit younger than I, and a little farther along dwelt Curt Offen with his divorced mother and younger brother. In those days a divorcee was unusual — Curt and his brother were the only children of divorced parents that I knew. Other than that difference, we had a number of things in common.

Curt Offen and I were in the same third grade class at Israel Putnam School on Broad Street, neither of us could abide our younger brothers, we got on very well and, most important from my point of view, he was a good listener.

Curt and I usually walked together to school, nearly a mile from my house. Often Jackie went with us. We three used to pass the time with stories — I would tell them, they would pay close attention, occasionally asking a question or, perhaps, making a comment. As I recall, those tales followed the models of the serial movie adventures we watched Saturdays at the old Capitol Theatre downtown, on the corner of Pratt and East Main, but the plots and characterizations were my own.

The route we took to school was capable of variation, and it could be full of adventure. There was the shortcut through an empty lot haunted by a great Dane — a gentle dog, but who was to know or care when it was easily twice your own size and came upon you silently and suddenly? There was the corner where the bully lived in a tenement house at Ann and Broad — I recollect the time when I'd had enough of being terrorized by him, picked up a stone, and threw it through his window when he ducked behind the railing of his porch three storeys up.

There was the candy store in the middle of Ann Street that sold colored sugar buttons on strips of paper and chewy Jujube hats; the drug store around the corner of Ann on Broad where, at the soda fountain, one discovered the sybaritic delights of chocolate ice cream sodas made with vanilla ice cream.

Sometimes Curt and I would take a route that avoided the streets, following instead a strip of brush and woods filled with the fiery October foliage of sumac and oak and the thin gray trunks of ironwood trees. Once when we were approaching the back yard of his house through this waste land, Curt picked up a broken glass phone pole insulator. Offhandedly he cocked his arm, threw his missile, and screamed. When I asked what was the matter, he stood silent for a moment to show me that the entire pad of the index finger of his right hand was missing, the blood pouring onto the ground. He began to scream again and went dashing off through the woods, as did I.

When I got home I said nothing to my parents about what had happened, perhaps on the theory that silence might keep me from trouble, though I'd done nothing wrong except come home through the woods, a practice of which our mothers did not much approve. But even silence couldn't save me. Soon there was a knock on the door and I was summoned to meet someone from the hospital or the doctor's office who wanted me to go with him back into the woods to look for the insulator and the missing part of Curt's finger. They thought that perhaps they could sew it back on.

I returned to the scene with extreme reluctance. I showed the young man where the accident had happened, and we scuffed about, turning over leaves and branches with the toes of our shoes. I had mixed feelings about finding what we were looking for, to say the least, but we did find it, still attached to the chunk of glass that had torn it off. Our effort proved to be useless, however, for we were too late. That part of Curt was dead for good and couldn't be made to live again.

I recall two — no, three accidents of my own in the Curtis Street house. Once I was running my tricycle around the living-room, I guess it was, where my mother was stretching curtains on a rack that had pinpoints sticking out all along the rectangular frame. I ran into the bottom of the frame. The needles punctured a row of bloody dots across my forehead just above my eyes. On another occasion I was knocked down in the schoolyard and split my scalp.

There was so much hemorrhaging I was sent home for the rest of the day. But the wound of which I was proud is the one I still call my "war wound." Curt and I used to play plane spotters in my room. I had bought a cardboard plane identification kit and altitude estimator at Kresge's or Woolworth's Five and Ten-Cent Store. It had a series of holes you could look through to see a plane flying past, and judging from the size of the hole into which the plane fitted best, you were supposed to be able to tell how high it was flying.

The kit also had plane silhouettes of all Axis and Allied aircraft, and you were supposed to compare what you saw with these outlines. I kept the kit in the drawer of an oak table near the window of my bedroom. Once when we heard a plane I made a dash for the open drawer, slipped and fell, cutting my arm just beneath the elbow, rather nastily, on the edge of the drawer. Again, lots of blood, but this time the wound, when it healed, left a visible scar.

My family lived on Curtis Street for two years or a little over, one of our longest terms of rental before my father's parishioners, the First Italian Baptist Church of Meriden, built the parsonage we moved into when I was in the seventh grade. The farmhouse was my favorite house, the street my favorite neighborhood, even though I was allergic to chicken feathers and dust and often had asthma attacks. I can recall all sorts of vivid scenes from those days, as for instance when some baby chicks found their way into a pig pen, were torn apart and eaten alive before my terrified stare. There was the night we were awakened by sirens and fire trucks roaring through our front yard to get to the chicken houses which were blazing in the darkness, sending up clouds of burned-feather-reeking smoke against the stars; the day I missed my cat, Bozo, and was reluctantly told, eventually, that a horse had stepped on him.

Still, I loved the place. I associate the now-banned smell of burning autumn leaves with Curtis Street. It was there that we children roasted corn and potatoes on cool summer evenings in pits dug in the earth — I never since have eaten potatoes that tasted so good. And it was there that Curt and I first made cornsilk pipes out of horse chestnuts. One day several years later, after we had moved away from Curtis Street, my mother caught me in the bathroom smoking cornsilk in a pipe I had hollowed out of a horse chestnut. I don't recall what I used for a stem. She was quite upset, of course, and she tried to extract from me a promise that I'd never smoke again.

I wasn't willing to go that far. I promised her that I wouldn't smoke until my sixteenth birthday, and I kept that promise. But on May 2, 1950 — my sixteenth natal celebration — I went down to Whelan's drug store on the corner of Colony Street and West Main. I looked over their stock, selected a Yello-Bowl that looked exactly like a horse chestnut, and a can of Holiday Pipe Tobacco. I went home, sat on the back porch, filled my new pipe and lit it. I was puffing away when my mother opened the back door, saw what I was doing, and went back inside, closing the screen door quietly.

That was it. She didn't argue with me about it. I'd kept my promise, and that was all she could ask. I smoked a pipe until I was in my early fifties, but I have for many years now been a non-smoker. Nevertheless, I still love the smell of pipe smoke, and I still own that first pipe I bought at Whelan's.

When my parents broke the news to me that we were moving from Curtis Street, it was with trepidation, and they were right to be apprehensive. They locked me in the hall to muffle my amazing fit of rage. I roared till everything turned white; I kicked the closed door until my father, usually the mildest of men, grew wrathful himself and opened it to face the berserker that was his elder son. I have never forgiven them for taking me away from the farmhouse on Curtis Street. I wanted to stay there the rest of my life.

When I grew a bit older and could ride a bike, I would sometimes go back to visit the old neighborhood, to see Jackie or Curt, Lindsey Churchill or John Molloy. Once when I returned the gang got together in Jackie's back yard. Someone had a live .22 caliber shell, and I thought I knew what to do with it. I put it on a stone, aimed it at a backstop rock, which I figured would stop the flight of the bullet, and began to pound the shell with a third rock. The other boys hid behind trees but stuck their heads out to watch.

Sometimes you wonder how so many kids survive to grow up. I discovered how stupid I'd been when the powder exploded, the bullet hit the backstop and ricocheted, whizzing past my ear, dirling in the air, setting my eardrum to vibrating. I can still hear the sound of that bullet when I think about it. Curt and Jackie behind the trees were equally fortunate that afternoon. Needless to say, we never told our parents how close they'd come to losing a child.

I ran into Curt again the first day of high school. I asked to look at his finger — it still had a notch in it the whole length of the knuckle. He was now quite a lot larger than I — heftier, taller, wearing a crew cut. He never became a member of our science-fiction reading club cum secret society, The Fantaseers, whose women's auxiliary was the backward-reading Reesatnafs; nor was he really one of the amalgamated co-ed crowd, The Fantatnafs, but he was a baritone, and I was a second tenor, in the Meriden High School Special Chorus.

In the high school we were incredibly fortunate in so many of our teachers, a good number of whom had been educated in such nearby places as Yale and Wesleyan. Not the least of these fine educators was our chorus director, Mr. Parisi, known as Tony even to the students, who all but idolized him. He directed not only the Special Chorus, but the Men's Glee Club and the Women's Choir as well, and there is a picture in our yearbook *The Annual* for 1952 of a select group of Glee Clubbers, The Octet, standing around or leaning on a piano as Tony plays for us. Curt and I were members, as were Chuck Verba and another, younger, Tony Perone.

It was Curt's idea that we further subdivide and become a barbershop quartet. He knew the proprietor of a sporting goods store, Al's Sportland. He got Al to sponsor us, that is, buy us music, and so we became The Sportlanders Quartet. We all had after school jobs. Until he went to work as a pump jockey at Barney's Service Station in South Meriden and I got fired, Curt and I, and Bill Burns as well, worked at

Kresge's, they as stock clerks and I as a busboy at the fountain. So Chuck, Curt, Tony, and I saved our money and bought white shirts and maroon trousers, bow ties, handkerchiefs, and armbands.

We began to line up singing dates in the area, and Tony Parisi also got us engagements. I recall once when the Chorus went to a Veteran's hospital in Newington to entertain the fallen troops. During a break, or while another act was performing, the Sportlanders went outdoors for air.

We took a walk around the grounds and came unexpectedly upon someone thrashing about in the underbrush, making horrible gasping sounds. We investigated and found one of the patients on the ground dying. Air was whistling in and out of a hole in his throat. One of us went running to get an orderly while the rest of us watched in fascinated horror at the last throes of this hero of the late War.

When the orderly arrived he said, "Oh, it's just Joe. He's drunk."

"What's wrong with his throat?"

"Tracheotomy. He's got a valve there that he has to hold to talk. He's too drunk to be able to do it. Come on, Joe," he said, "time to go beddy-bye."

We were embarrassed and relieved. Greatly relieved.

Even this experience was worth being a member of a quartet. There is nothing like barbershopping. Many people think it is a gauche and sentimental form of music. If the lyrics were the only thing you listened to, this assessment might be correct, but the words are nothing. It's the harmony, the chords that count. Up till the last few years I still went to barbershop chorus in Oswego where I teach college. Our director was a Ph.D. in philosophy, and, until he moved out of town, our arranger was another. I must admit, even I find something incongruous, when I think of it, about barbershop philosophers.

The key of a quartet is the tenor who, in effect, sings alto. A good tenor will have a falsetto that doesn't crack when he descends into normal range, that is clear and true. Such a one was the younger Tony. I sang lead. I'm not much of a musician, but I could handle the melody all right as a general rule. My voice was sturdy, and the other parts could hang onto it easily.

Curt was the baritone. This part is the hardest of the four to sing, because there is no logic in it. The baritone fills in; sometimes he is singing lead-range, bass-range, and even, on rare occasions, tenor-range notes. The baritone must be an excellent musician who can hold his part through sheer memory against the harmonic pull of the other three singers, but he can never dominate. He must swell or diminish whenever the particular song requires it. Curt was a fine baritone.

We started out with Chuck as our bass. The bass is the foundation of the quartet. He supports the other three on the root of his voice. Chuck was the root, I was the trunk; Curt was the branches, and Tony the leaves. Our goal, when we sang, was the same as that of any quartet: to "ring" a chord. This phenomenon can only be described, never wholly understood in any way other than through performance. If one wishes to listen to chords ringing he can do so by getting a compact disk of "The Music Man" and listening to the old Buffalo Bills singing "Lida Rose."

When everything is going just right — when the four voices are the perfect blend of pitch, tone, balance, dynamics — then a quartet can ring a chord. The "ring" is a fifth voice, a vibrating overtone that can be heard hovering somewhere in the air over the singers. It sends a shiver down four spines when it happens. The hair on the nape of your neck stands on end, your eardrums dirl and your lobes tingle — you can feel the tingle in all your extremities, in fact.

Ringing a chord is a visionary experience. People stay barbershoppers so that they can have this experience now and again — it doesn't happen all the time, nor even often. The Sportlanders got good enough to ring a chord on occasion.

The existence of The Sportlanders was soon threatened, however. I never did understand the situation, about which Chuck did not speak, but evidently his girlfriend's mother objected to him strongly, for some reason, and threatened to pull her out of school and send her off somewhere. I guess the girl's parents wanted Chuck out of town, rather than as a son-in-law. Being, as it were, a Knight in Shining Armor, Chuck voluntarily left school himself and went into the service so that Sheila could finish her senior year at Meriden High. Wisely, in my opinion, he chose the Navy. We needed to get a new bass, and so we acquired Ed.

Ed was an excellent musician too. After his education he went into the Army and became a member of the Army Band in Washington, D.C. Years later Jean and I ran into someone who knew Ed, and he told us a horrendous story: Ed had come down with some sort of incurable disease that was progressively debilitating. His doctors held out no hope for him. One day he was languishing on the sofa in his home when an acquaintance of his wife, a nutritionist, came for a visit. At a glance she identified Ed's disease. "Why don't you take vitamins?" she asked.

Ed said there was no cure for his disease. The nutritionist snorted. "Of course there is, it's just a vitamin deficiency. Doctors hate to believe things can be cured with vitamins." Then and there she wrote out a list of the nutriments he ought to take and Ed began the regimen. He was soon back on his feet. Within a year he was completely well and furious with the medical profession. He wrote a book. The person who told me this story handed me a copy of the paperback Ed had written about his ordeal and cure, but I never read it. That was the year we had watched my father-in-law die of a truly incurable disease, cancer, and I had no heart to read anything medical.

The cancer had started as prostate cancer. Dad Houdlette never treated it, nor told anyone in the family about it until it was too late and had spread up his spinal column. About the same time I was myself diagnosed with prostatitis, and I asked my doctor how long I was going to have the condition.

"It's chronic," he said. "You'll have it the rest of your life. But you can alleviate it by taking vitamin C." I began taking C, and the condition did improve. Then Marie Delemarre said she'd been told zinc was good, too, so I started taking zinc — and the condition improved even further. Jean said that E was supposed to help, so I began taking E, and the condition completely disappeared! Then I found there was a commercial formula called "Z-BEC." For years now I've been taking it, and at my annual physical just this year I was told by the same doctor that had diagnosed my condition that there is no sign of it. That's a long aside, but it tends to support Ed's story.

The quartet had a trick we liked to play, especially when we were attending meetings of the Silver City Chapter of S.P.E.B.S.Q.S.A., the Society for the Preservation and Encouragement of Barber Shop Quartet Singing in America. We would pitch our songs high — Tony would sing soprano; I would tilt at alto; Curt filled in with tenor, and Ed raised his voice into baritone range. This could be truly an amazing thing to hear, especially when there was total silence and we were singing quietly and sweetly. Then, when we rang a chord, it would practically lift your scalp off.

Except, of course, when I had hay fever. Then everything went to hellandgone. Unfortunately, I got hay fever fairly often — I seemed to be allergic to everything, though I discovered the condition years later to be largely psychosomatic. As soon as I made that conscious, my allergies largely disappeared. Unfortunately, when we went down to audition for the Ted Mack Amateur Hour in New York City, I had not yet made the roots of my adolescent miseries conscious. Better not to dwell on that failure. We never appeared on the new medium, television, though we did sing once on the local radio station, WMMW.

Fantaseers

We sang everywhere we went. We would sometimes just get into a car and go somewhere, singing, even in the middle of the night. We sang at school functions, at parties, at Elks Club meetings.

Sometimes on a hot summer day we would head for the Connecticut shore and the beach cottage of one of the gang, Paul or Alice, for on these occasions the other three members of the quartet became honorary Fantatnafs. We would sing in the sand and draw a crowd.

In 1952, the year Curt and I graduated from Meriden High, the Sportlanders spent a week, between graduation and my reporting for Naval duty, at Laurel Music Camp in the hills of western Connecticut. When we arrived at the registration table we paid our fees with a bagful of silver dollars and sang, "As a silver dollar goes from hand to hand, a woman goes from man to man." We were, of course, in those pre-feminist days, a romantic sensation on the spot, but barbershoppers no longer sing that song.

Don Craig, our chorus director, gave me a solo to sing in "Summertime," and he even let the quartet record a song. Unfortunately, in the latter performance my allergies were in evidence, and I have a cassette recorder now that makes recordings two or three hundred times better than the "professional" equipment that they used to tape our renditions then, so I have no proof The Sportlanders ever rang a chord.

That was the climax of our collective career. For a few years we got together now and then when I could get liberty or leave to come home at the same time that Curt was back from college and the other two guys, still in high school, were available as well. Those reunions grew fewer and fewer, and we grew rustier and rustier. Still, we looked forward to the next time chance might throw us together.

Then, when Jean and I were in our thirties, living in Central New York, and Curt was a transport pilot in the Air Force, he died. We heard two stories about how it happened; first, that he succumbed overseas in an allergic reaction to a shot for malaria. But once, when I was visiting Meriden, I stopped in to see Bill, the proprietor of Barney's Service Station on Hanover Street in South Meriden where Curt had worked for a while. "Hell," Bill told me, "he didn't die from no shot! He choked to death on a piece of meat."

I never did find out which was true. I wrote his mother, but she didn't reply. We got a formal thank-you from his wife, whom we'd never met. But it doesn't really matter, for dead is dead. The quartet can never sing again in any case; that possibility simply no longer exists. While we were both in the Navy I ran into Chuck once, in the Philippines, of all places, but I lost touch with him, for many years with Ed and "young" Tony, too.

One weekend in the late 'seventies Jean and I went back home for a visit. Though a passing dread lies waiting for us when we double in our track, that time I picked up the phone and called Tony Parisi, our chorus director, who had long-since retired as a teacher. Hearing him speak, I felt relieved to a degree, for he sounded as he had used to. I had brunch with him next day at his house, served by his wife "Tata," and, hard as it may be to believe, he was in fact exactly the same as I remembered him. I'd played a hunch and, this once, had won. We spent a splendid afternoon, quipping and reminiscing.

Down in his den he had pictures of The Sportlanders on his desk and on the wall as well — photographs, the cartoon drawn by the young Tony that I'd forgotten, but that with the others I'd autographed. The elder Tony tried to give it to me, but I couldn't accept it. I came near once again, though, to hearing those close chords, spellbinding when we blended into a single voice of chiming parts. And then I walked away. The only chord that rings now is this one, the close harmony of recall that dirls in the night air.

THE MUTABLE PAST

The vacant lot where we North Third Street kids played softball on those sunny New England summer days was full of trees, and it was small. When we wanted to play hardball we went down the street, to West Main, crossed, walked a hundred feet or so to our left, and turned into the Lincoln Junior High School driveway. The school had a big playing field, but we were likely there to run into other young folk from adjacent neighborhoods, so we tended to stay within a two-block radius of our homes.

We were quite a crowd, mostly of an age. Bob Strauss lived across the street from me. He was a couple of years older, and he was practicing to become the New England fife-and-drum corps snare drum champion in a few years. Next door to him lived Phil Reilly who, like me, was in the sixth grade, but in parochial rather than public school. Down the street were the Gaffney brothers, Marty and Billy, a couple of tough, skinny kids, and across from them lived the Muravnick sisters, Janice and Pat. Janice played ball with us sometimes, for she was a tomboy. On Second Street there were the Carlson brothers, a couple of hard cases in my opinion, but I never really had trouble with them, though I recall worrying about it a good deal. Kenny Noack lived on the corner between my house and the vacant lot. Just at the edge of the lot there stood a mysterious shack. It appeared to have been a store because it had plate-glass windows, but one made out shapes through them with difficulty, they were so covered with grit.

When we had finished playing our game among the trees that were our bases and that turned the contest into an object lesson in ricochet physics, we would gather up our gear, such as it was — a ball, a bat or two, but hardly ever a glove — and head for home. On the way we might stop to peer in through the windows of the shack, the sun at our backs glinting off the dark glass. We would push our faces up as close as we could and use both hands to shield our eyes. Even so, all we could make out inside were the outlines of what appeared to be some machines.

Before we left we would rattle the padlock on the splinter-dry front door and speculate. Some of our guesses were fantastic, others more mundane. One theorized that the shack might be a rendezvous for spies — the Second World War had not long been over — who came only at night. Or it was an old machine shop left over from the war when many of our parents had been engaged in carrying two jobs at the same time in little war industries that had sprung up everywhere. Then our interest ebbed, and we forgot to think about it.

One summer after school had let out for good I took to getting up early — who knows why? — and hanging around the street while my slugabed friends kept their dreams alive. I recall one morning when I walked out the front door onto the big front porch, down the wooden stairs, then down the flight of concrete steps to the sidewalk, for our house sat up on a bank. I stood with my hands in my pocket, my eyes drinking in the early cool beneath the elms that used to line our avenues, sunlight mottling the road like the design of a Moorish carpet. I looked down the street, then up the street, and I spotted a battered prewar pickup truck sitting at the curb in front of the old shack. I noticed that the awning was down, something I hadn't seen before, and then from the doorway there emerged a man carrying a couple of what appeared to be boxes. He ducked under the awning, lifted his burden over the tailgate, arranged them, then turned and went back in.

Naturally, I sauntered up the block as quickly as possible without, I hoped, appearing to hurry, and soon I was standing where I could see inside. I could hear the machines running. When my eyes adjusted to the inner dusk, I saw the man — he was a big man — lifting milk cans and pouring their contents into a hopper. The machine rattled and ratcheted, bottles clattered as they were filled with white, foamy milk. The man was busy, for he was handling all the manual chores including putting bottles onto the conveyer belt, taking them off at the other end, and racking them in the crates. I waited until I was sure the milkman had seen me, then imperceptibly I edged closer to the center of action.

I don't recall how near I managed to get the first day, or the second, or even exactly when he spoke to me, but eventually I did get the idea he had no objection to my being there, or even to my lending a hand, such as it was, upon occasion. In fact, rather than words I recall mainly a friendly silence between us. I do remember that finally he asked me if I'd like to go out on his route with him, and I said yes. "Go ask your mom if it's all right," he said, and I did.

For some reason my mother agreed. She came down and spoke with him, but she must also have done some checking when I told her about the big man bottling milk in the mornings, and perhaps it was even she who told me the man's name was Walsh. At any rate, there came the morning when I helped Mr. Walsh load up and got into the seat beside him. Soon we were rattling around on the outskirts of town towards Wallingford and Yalesville — the bottles rattled with the old pickup, and our teeth did likewise, for there was little left of the suspension and nothing of the shock absorbers, if we had any.

The mornings passed pleasantly. We would go to the side or back door of a house to leave one or two or three of those old-fashioned round, long-necked bottles on the stoop. The cream would have risen to the top pretty well by the time we'd delivered the milk, and I could imagine the people in the house doing what my mother did, that is, carefully pouring some off the top into a morning cup of coffee. Before I drank a glass of such milk at home or poured it onto my cereal I would always shake the bottle to distribute the cream. Now I can't drink milk at all, not even the processed sort, for I can't digest it — nor can most adults, though not many people seem to know it. I should have realized this sooner because Bernie Jurale, my high school chemistry and home room teacher, kept telling us over and over that it was so. We students thought he was a crank, and that's why, when I developed an ulcer during my Navy days after high school, I drank lots of milk because doctors said it was good for the condition. How can doctors be so wrong so often? It was the worst thing they could have prescribed. Back in the 1940s, however, who knew these things? What I remember is the creamy, delicious taste of whole milk and, in the winter, the bottles of milk standing outside the back door with their caps raised into the air on a column of cream, for as the bottle froze its contents expanded. That's a sight no child will see again; these days, if people drink milk at all, it's skim milk, for milkfat is supposed to be bad for our cholesterol levels. Back then you got skim milk by skimming off all of the head of cream, but the resulting liquid tasted like blue chalk water, and it still does.

Sometimes one of our customers would open the door as we were making our delivery — a woman in a housecoat or a man dressed for work but without his jacket on. They might say, "Hello, Mr. Walsh," or "Good morning," and call my friend by his first name — was it Ed? Jim? And he would nod and smile. Then we'd get back into the truck and be on our way. When we had finished the route it would still be early. My friends would just be getting up and coming outdoors. Bob or Phil might see me waving to Mr. Walsh as he drove away. Soon we would begin our long summer day of ball or exploring or playing war or cops and robbers.

It was in 1959, when Jean and I were living in Storrs, Connecticut, and I was attending the university there that my mother sent me the newspaper obituary of a local man named "Big Ed" Walsh. Mom May was always sending me clippings from the local papers — I'd left a paper trail of her gleanings completely around the world, for she had kept me apprised of local affairs all the while I had been in the Navy — through boot camp in Maryland, my first assignment in Norman, Oklahoma, the two years I'd spent aboard the aircraft carrier *Hornet* while she circled the globe, and my fourth year as a Yeoman in Arlington, Virginia, at the Bureau of Naval Personnel where I became the most famous and mythical of sailors, the fellow who sat on the shore duty list.

I don't know what led me to believe that the subject of the obituary was my milkman friend. Was it something my mother wrote in her letter? I can't find it in my files. Was it the picture that ran with the death notice? Was it merely a conclusion that I'd jumped to? I'd had some suspicions before then that Mr. Walsh had been a ballplayer, but in my childhood I was, and am still, a pure Yankee fan. I knew little or nothing of any other team except the Yankees' archrival Boston Red Sox.

Oh, I'd had an experience with the Philadelphia Athletics who'd come to town to play an exhibition game with our semi-pro Insilco team at Insilco Field (now a shopping mall) sponsored by the International Silver Company that gave our town, Meriden, the sobriquet "Silver City." If I'm not mistaken, Connie Mack had once managed the Meriden team. I went to that game on the day that had been named for him, and I saw Mr. Mack with my own eyes, but I was not otherwise one of the cognoscenti of the ballpark. Whatever it was, something convinced me that I'd been delivering milk in Connecticut with Big Ed Walsh, a Hall-of-Fame player for the Chicago White Sox from 1904 to 1916, and a one-season forty-game winner at a time when giants bestrode the mound and raced around the diamond track. Big Ed had been born in 1881, so when we were both residents of the same town he was about sixty-five years of age. He'd spent one year, 1917, with the Boston National League team before he retired at the age of thirty-six. He had thus been doing other things for twenty-nine years before I rode my summer milk route with my friend.

I've been living in Central New York State for many years, now, and many years back I drove down to Cooperstown with another elderly friend, Charlie Davis, who had been a jazz-band leader during the years of Ed Walsh's early retirement. I used to get a bang out of thinking that Ed must have heard Charlie's famous jazz composition "Copenhagen" many times on his crystal set. Charlie and I went winding down through the hills and picnicked in a lakeside park there in Cooperstown. We attended a meeting of the New York State Folklore Association where Charlie was a featured speaker, having turned into a writer and publisher in one of his several incarnations. And then we went over to the Baseball Hall of Fame where I looked up Big Ed.

There he was, on the wall with the other titans of bat and mound. I tried to get into a suitable mood of awe as I stood there, but had no success at it. All I could see reflected in what I perceived to be memory's lake was a dusty road unwinding before the beat-up hood of an old pickup, and a bottle of milk that wore a crown of cream. Later, I wrote a prize-winning poem about those summer mornings and my friend, Mr. Walsh, and later still I did a short nostalgic piece for a national magazine which brought me letters and phone calls from all sorts of people who remembered Big Ed Walsh and the Meriden of my childhood as vividly as I did. Jim Masterson, a high school classmate, phoned to chat about it, and so did our choral director at M. H. S., Tony Parisi, but we weren't at home for his call so my son, Christopher, took the message and relayed it to Maine where we were vacationing.

John P. Kiley, Sr., wrote from Derby, Connecticut. "I organized and was chairman of the Naugatuck Valley Old Time Athletes," he informed

Fantaseers

me. "We were fortunate to have Big Ed as the featured speaker both in 1950 and 1951. The Hotel Clark (since razed) in Derby was filled to the walls because Big Ed was coming and all the Old Timers (some in their 80's...) had a chance to meet, listen to, and shake hands with him. As the chairman I can say it was one of the happiest occasions. I still have scrap books of the events and will pass them on to my son and grandsons. I am eighty-eight, so I remember the Chicago White Sox when we listened on ticker tape or radio. I have pitching tips written by Big Ed and also his autograph."

Another who responded was Warren F. Gardner, who was Editor of *The Morning Record* of Meriden for many years, including that couple of years when I worked as high school correspondent for the paper and as cub reporter and morgue clerk as well (the "morgue" is the library of clippings on people and events that all newspapers maintain). Warren wrote, "I was delighted to read your little piece about Big Ed Walsh.... You were lucky to know him. I knew he was a baseball player of repute, but until I read your column I did not know that he ran the dairy on North Third Street.

"I remember the dairy well, of course. I was born in 1909 in the second floor apartment of the house at 45 North Fourth Street. Father owned the house. He rented the downstairs apartment. We lived there until I was age 16, then moved to Carpenter Avenue.

"So I grew up on the West Side and loved it. We had good neighbors; I can remember many of them. We had milk delivered to our back door in the glass bottles you mentioned. No such thing as homogenizing in those days, either of milk or men.

"On occasion, if we ran short of milk or mother wanted some cream, I was sent to get it at Walsh's dairy, often bringing it home in the small pail I carried with me. Whoever waited on me dipped it out of the vat. In those days milkmen made deliveries by horse and wagon. There was a barn in the rear of the little milk station where the horse was stabled. On one occasion my father sprained his wrist badly while trying to crank the open Ford Model T touring car we had. Dr. E. W. Smith advised a poultice made of hay seeds soaked in hot water and wrapped around the wrist. Where to get hay seeds? Mr. Walsh's hay loft, of course. So father and I went there, and with Walsh's permission scooped up about a pint of seeds from the bottom of the mow."

But the nostalgia piece that Warren Gardner and John Kiley read and responded to also brought me a letter from a man now living in Massachusetts, Raymond E. Burke, who said that, although many things in my essay were accurate, the central fact was not a fact at all, for I had confused Big Ed Walsh with another man named Walsh, proprietor for many years of Walsh's Dairy on North Third Street. Mr. Burke wrote that "The man that ran J. J. Walsh Dairy was James J. Walsh...and [his] home was on Columbus Avenue." According to him, by 1949 the dairy no longer existed because it was "...closed and Walsh sold his milk route to another milk dealer...in the middle '40's." How can the past transform itself like that? How can one remember things that never existed? For I did a lot of checking, particularly through Warren Gardner, and discovered that Mr. Burke was correct. Warren wrote, "It looks like a case of mistaken identity. Today I checked several Meriden city directories from about 1930 to 1950. The earlier directories gave no occupation for Edward A. Walsh, merely his home address, until 1950 when the listing read: 'Edward A. Walsh, caretaker Broad Brook reservoir h[ome] Finch av[enue] bey[ond] town line.'"

I recall that the obituary my mother sent me had mentioned that Big Ed was the caretaker of a reservoir in Meriden, and Mr. Burke said that he and his father had struck up an acquaintance with the former baseball great when they went fishing there. The obituary never mentioned a milk route, but I had nevertheless been convinced somehow that my summer morning companion had been a retired ball-player.

Fantaseers

In one of my forays back to my home town I had myself acquired a copy of *The Meriden Directory*, vol. 73 for 1949. I have it before me now, and under "W" it has exactly the entries that Warren Gardner quoted, and it has no listing for the dairy itself, thus confirming Mr. Burke's claim that by then it had been sold. Warren tried to make me feel better about my error. He wrote, "I have no doubt whatsoever that you believed the man you helped deliver milk was 'Big Ed' himself. As a boy I delivered the *Morning Record* to a Pilkington family at the east end of North Avenue. Charlie Pilkington, a young son in the family, was in the news as a promising young amateur prize fighter. He and Kid Kaplan, who went on to win the world's championship for his weight, were contemporaries. I always hoped that Charlie, who was a hero in the neighborhood, at least among the boys, would answer the door when I collected for the paper, but he never did, and I never saw him. I never saw 'Big Ed' Walsh either."

Lewis Turco in his office aboard
the USS Hornet, 1953

PAUL

Paul Wiese, my friend from junior high and high school, is dead now in middle age of throat cancer. When Paul disappeared from view into the streets of Chicago his sister Alice, according to the grapevine, left New England to find him, discovered him ill and alone, and brought him back to our home town to die. In his last days — I'm told, for I've not lived in Meriden for many years — he might be glimpsed wandering about, perhaps on West Main Street where his father's Butter and Egg Store had been when we were teenagers. Next door there'd been a high school hangout, a soda salon called The Katt Brothers, run by two men named Alfred and Clarence Katt. It and the market were fronted in shiny black stone — marble or a reasonable facsimile thereof.

I did very little lounging about in Katt's. It wasn't my milieu — something too arty or ritzy about it, not comfortable. I think it was mostly girls who sat in the booths sipping chocolate ice-cream sodas or dabbing at sundaes, and Paul had never been much interested in girls.

His father next door was a thin, small man who did a fair amount of smiling. Paul and I would stop in after school sometimes to say hello. Besides its stone front the shop shared with Katt's, I felt, a sort of alien ambience, a bit too much like New York City, in my naive notion of style. In the malted milk palace I seemed to feel pressure to be clever and witty — I didn't mind being those things, but I minded the constraint. In the store Paul and I were sharp among the cheeses, and we were rewarded with his father's silent and squinting laughter.

Paul and I had met the first day of the eighth grade at Lincoln Junior High, located in those days of the late 1940s not far from the corner of Windsor Avenue. Across West Main Street, Windsor Avenue should have continued; instead, the thoroughfare became North Third Street. In the fifth and sixth grades I had lived with my family on North Third, but then we'd moved to the other end of Windsor which was, now that I think of it, only one enormous block long. It was broken by no other street, except an alley called Quinlan Avenue, until it got to Springdale Avenue where my father's church stood on a corner that separated the Catholic Italian section of town from the miscellaneous neighborhood of Windsor.

My initial acquaintance with Paul had lasted only a week or two — the first two weeks of the eighth grade. I was to be sent away to attend Suffield Academy at the end of that period, but my father had insisted that I begin school locally to kill the time until the later opening of the prep school which was located thirty or forty miles away.

What a fortnight that was for Paul and me! There was some strange chemistry between us. We felt in one another's character a kind of daredeviltry, and we vied with one another to see which of us had more of it.

The reputedly meanest teacher in the school was a math instructor, Herman Dressler, but we actually fired paper clips at him as he stood at the blackboard with his back to us. Worse, we got away with it. He never said anything to the class, even when the clips bounced off the board and landed at his feet. Dressler's non-reaction is one of the many minor mysteries of a lifetime, and I have spent the odd moment wondering about it over the years.

I remember nothing else specific from that brief period, but I do recall the heady frenzy I felt while it was passing, and I assume Paul felt it too. Then it was over and I went away for two years, which was all my father could afford, even with the courtesy ministerial scholarship he had arranged for me, for Suffield Academy was at that time a Baptist-affiliated, run-down, four-building outfit in a very pretty old Connecticut town. I was told that I was being sent away to get the best education available, but many years later my brother Gene told me it was to save his life.

I wonder if I can calculate how many schools I went to before my parents shipped me out of town entirely: for kindergarten I went to the Lewis Avenue school, a very long block and a half away from the church. Somewhere later along the line the city sold it to St. Mary's church to be used as a parochial school. That year we lived on the corner of Lewis and Springdale.

But it would be pointless and boring to recite a litany of the institutions of my primary education, for even Lincoln and Meriden High no longer exist. They have disappeared into the mists of adolescence with the physical plants of most of the other schools I attended. Let me say merely that I attended nearly every grammar school in town except Samuel Huntington, the one my future wife was attending, because, the church having no parsonage, and my mother not being able to get along with anyone at all, landlords in particular, we moved nearly every year.

Two weeks of the eighth grade, and I left Paul and all that behind. At Suffield I spent one year in the Lower School and another as a freshman in the Upper School, then my father ran out of money and I had to go home for high school. It was the old story over again — I had just made friends with the boys at the Academy, had even been elected president of the freshman class, and now I was to be pulled out and sent to a place full of strangers.

But there, instead, were all those people with whom I had gone to school all over town! And there was Paul from Lincoln Junior High, in my home room, no less! There he stood, all five-feet-four of him, his slightly bowed legs, angular Aryan face and Irish coloring — deep blue eyes, red hair, freckles, the lips full and quick to curl into a satyr's sneer — there was an edge to his humor, something perhaps a bit too sharp and offbeat about it.

One of the first things we did was to invent the initials "H. P. N. Y.," which we plastered everywhere in the school and even in store windows downtown — in Paul's dad's place, in Kresge's five and dime were I worked as a busboy, in Golab's Jewelry Store next to the Palace Theater, in Molloy's Stationers and Jepson's Bookstore. We had everyone in school asking what the letters stood for, or when whatever they stood for was supposed to happen. We told no one they meant nothing.

We soon had our home room, which contained the nucleus of what would become "The Fantaseers," organized — when Mr. Jurale, the chemistry teacher, came in we all rose, saluted, and intoned, "Hail, Chief!" The salute was Paul's — a salute from the recently past Second World War. Paul liked to think of himself as a "German sympathizer," which no one took seriously. He didn't know enough, I think, to understand that he was more a prewar Bohemian of degenerate persuasion than anything else.

My mother, not surprisingly, took a dislike to Paul and wouldn't for a while allow him inside the house after she found the hypodermic needle he'd asked me to keep for him. He had never used it to my knowledge, nor had I — I didn't even understand what my mother was upset about at the time. I thought Paul just wanted to have it because he'd heard it was illegal, and it gave him a kick to think that we were doing something risky.

He also talked me into taking German rather than Spanish, which would have been much the easier of the two languages to learn, especially inasmuch as I heard Italian every week in church when my father preached dual sermons. We didn't speak it at home, of course, my mother being half Yankee and half Danish.

Though Paul and I played Damon and Pythias for a while in our sophomore year, with Bill Burns as our Sancho Panza (if I may be allowed to mix a metaphor), it soon became evident that there was a rivalry between us as well. We were interested in the same clubs. In those days, when extracurricular activities counted almost more than grades did toward one's being accepted by colleges, one wished to be not merely a member of an organization, but an officer, preferably the president. We found ourselves running against one another on more than one occasion, and it became clear that I was going to win against him if for no other reason than that I knew more people than he did. Paul invented the solution — in those cases where we were in the same clubs, we would caucus and split the offices between us, thus avoiding head-to-head contests.

By the end of our sophomore year, even before our club, The Fantaseers, had made their mark, I was growing away from Paul. For one thing, he made me uneasy at times; for another, I had made a friend, Ray Staszewski, who shared with me the desire to become a writer, an ambition in which Paul had no interest — he intended to be a teacher. Paul, I know, was hurt by my swiftly developing friendship with Ray. From time to time his resentment began to take the form of practical jokes played on me, as for instance when he opened a can of shrimp and dumped them among the papers at the bottom of my messy locker. For days I didn't locate the source of the developing odor which eventually became truly horrendous, the ultimate stench!

I was not incapable of retaliation, however, and Paul was at last driven to take physical measures against me. He caught me one day kneeling to tie my shoe. He grabbed my hair and held my head down so that I couldn't rise. I became so furious that I painfully raised my head despite the thrust of his arm and glared at him. I warned him to let go or I'd kill him. My body was trembling with tension, and I doubled my fist in preparation to deliver an uppercut that would start literally from the floor, despite his superior position. I think he could feel it coming, because at the last moment he released me and walked away before I could get to my feet.

Though we maintained our relationship as Fantaseers after that, we did fewer and fewer things as a pair. When we were seniors our classmates hurt him deeply. He wanted to pull our old club officer-splitting device over two elections, those for Class Wit and Class Prankster, both of which would appear in *The Annual* for 1952, our yearbook. He was willing to concede the Wit to me, but he wanted the Prankster title.

There's a picture in *The Annual* — I made sure, as co-editor, that it got in — of Paul standing on the apron of the auditorium stage, dressed in a jester's motley outfit, cap and bells. I don't remember what drama production it was from. Paul's head is cocked and he is looking out at the audience with that worldly-innocent expression he so easily and deliberately affected. I agreed to stand back and not campaign for prankster, but Paul needn't have made me promise, for it did no good anyway — the class did as they wished. Paul was someone who could have used the ego boost a show of popularity would have given, and there was much to be said in support of his being the true class prankster, but there was in the end nothing that could be done about the vote.

And so we graduated. Paul went to New Britain State Teachers' College to major in education. Ray and I joined the Navy to qualify for the G. I. Bill, for neither of our families could afford to send us to school. My contacts with Paul became fewer and fewer. Once, in the spring of 1953 when I was stationed in Norman, Oklahoma — attached, I used to tell people who asked, to a fleet of prairie schooners — I sent him a horned toad in a Band-Aid box poked full of holes. He wrote me it had arrived in good condition, and he'd given it to a biology professor to put into a terrarium. I hope it was true — that ugly creature had been a pet I carried around in the pocket of my jumper for a while and fed on captured flies.

My mother was forever sending Jean and me clippings from *The Morning Record*, and one of them arrived when I was myself in College and Paul had graduated. He was engaged to a college classmate, they were planning to be married, and they would teach at the same school, or in the same school district. Then, somewhat later, another story caught up with us: Paul had been fired from his first job. "Morals" had been cited as the cause. We heard nothing more of his impending marriage.

Some years later — it must have been in 1968 or after — I was surprised by a phone call from him. He was dean of boys in a midwestern private school, and he had heard about a reference work I'd published, *The Book of Forms*. He asked why I hadn't sent him a copy. "I didn't know you were interested," I told him, but I'd be pleased to do so if he'd give me his address. I sent him an inscribed copy which he didn't acknowledge, and I never heard from him again.

Everything else we heard about Paul was through Marie Delemarre Ho, a classmate who, like Jean, had been a member of the Fantaseers' opposites, the feminine Reesatnafs. On our infrequent visits to Meriden from Oswego in Upstate New York Marie would run down the gossip about the gang and the class, with most of whom we had lost touch since we stopped going to reunions after the tenth anniversary of our graduation. Marie didn't know the details of how Paul had ended up on the streets of Chicago, but she saw him now and then in Meriden, obviously ill and dying.

I made no attempt to see him, and I'm not sure how I feel about that as I sit here writing. One ought to feel guilty, I suppose, under the circumstances. Marie felt that it would have cheered him up to see me, but I doubt it. I've visualized what it might have been like, and I think it would have been painful for both of us.

Fantaseers

When Burns showed up at my door in Oswego that recent summer after all those years, I asked him whether he'd seen Paul, for Bill had moved only as far as Wallingford, a stone's throw from Meriden. He said no, he hadn't.

Time had failed Paul early. The roots of that failure lay in our adolescence. Time was failing me, too, but still I had some, and I suspect it would have been alum and oil for each of us to look into the other's eyes. More bitter for him, perhaps, for the pity or sorrow or sadness I fear he would have read in my glances. Or possibly he simply would not have cared any longer, not have wished to look back into the downlands of years where the scattered seed of promise lay sprouting. The difference between then and now is in rue and hearts bane. It is in knowledge of the harvest.

Barbara Brooks, Lewis Turco, Nancy Lundquist, 1951

BURNS

Burns had the first television set in our gang. In 1949 Paul and I would go over to Burns' house to watch the few programs available: "Your Show of Shows," "The Milton Berle Show," and "professional" wrestling with Gorgeous George and others of less colorful ilk. Not that it mattered much on the fuzzy black and white screen.

Paul and I were sophomores in Meriden High and Burns was a year ahead of us. The 1951 *Annual* says that he was "...short, quiet, and witty...likes to read science fiction and is a fiend for chess and checkers...claims that French verbs are his worst enemy...hopes to attend business college after graduation." When he phoned me during the summer of 1991 I recognized his voice, though I hadn't heard it for nearly forty years, and when he stood in my livingroom in Oswego, New York, I recognized him. He'd filled out some, but he still looked like Burns.

"I married a girl from New Haven," he said. Not the New Haven just down the Wilbur Cross Parkway from Meriden, but the one in Upstate New York, not more than twenty miles from my home. "We've been coming up here for years. I've called you lots of times, but this is the first time you've answered."

I told him Jean and I spent most of our summers in Maine, and that it was a shame we couldn't have gotten together sooner. We sat and had a beer, chatting about old times and catching up on family matters. He had three kids, never went to any sort of college but was a paramedic for

Fantaseers

a while after the service, and wound up in Wallingford where he worked in a plant as a technician.

That business about his liking to read science fiction was a reference to our high school "science fiction reading club." "I've still got one of those Fantaseers cards," he said.

"So do I!"

"White lettering on black plastic?"

"Right."

I told him that one day a year or two ago I'd gone up to my garret study and begun to rummage around, just on the off-chance I'd made a folder of Fantaseer memorabilia. I checked my files and found the club's Constitution, a list of members, and a chronology of the events of the first eighteen months of our two and one-half year existence. On that occasion Jean had said, "It's a good thing you have the soul of a clerk." Not just the soul, which I'd inherited from my mother, but the training as well, thanks to the Navy.

The Fantaseers was formed in January of 1950 at a party held at the home of one of our classmates — I can't remember who that was now. The first of the four charter members was Peter, whose I. Q. tested out at 165. His entry in *The Annual* says, "'Goose' is one of the few students who owns a coveted berth in the National Honor Society...his weaknesses include movies and ping-pong [playing poker should also have been mentioned]...a strong player on the soccer team...will go to college and study engineering." He was voted "Most Likely to Succeed" in our senior year.

I'm listed next: "'Luigi'"— actually, my father's name "...a real personality...the co-Editor whose originality and hard work helped make this *Annual* possible...Lewis has brightened many a class with his endless supply of 'corn'...a sparkling tenor...would like to attend Bucknell University." Voted both "Class Prankster" and "Class Wit."

Lindsey is the third. He has no entry in the yearbook because he skipped his senior year, went to both Yale and Harvard on Ford Foundation Fellowships, skipping his master's degree and going right from his B. A. to his Ph. D. and becoming a famous academic in an esoteric branch of sociology.

Phineas, whose fate, although I've seen him once in a great while, I do not know, was the fourth. "'Phin,' the salesman par excellence...able manager of the basketball team...one really cannot appreciate 'Phin' without knowing him intimately...member of National Honor...another science-fiction advocate...UConn's gain will be our loss." Phineas had been my best friend during the year or so that my family had lived on Newton Street when I was in early grade school, but when we were reunited in high school he had no recollection of our earlier acquaintance.

The next member entered in the Constitution was Bill Burns who gave the Fantaseers their motto: "There's nothing like good clean fun, and this is nothing like it"; George Hangen was a Congregational minister's son; "One of the boss-men of the class...the competent and industrious co-editor of the 1951 *Annual*, who spent hours making this book possible...skilled pianist and member of Special Chorus...active member of the German Club...a debater...a man with a future" who followed in his father's clerical footsteps.

Pierre Bennerup was the son of a Danish nurseryman in Kensington, not far away down the Chamberlain Highway, and a French mother. He had no entry, either, because his family had moved out of Meriden before his senior year. He attended Princeton, worked in New York for many years in a wine importing company, if I'm not mistaken, and has now run the nursery for years since his father's death, having added two others to his properties.

Johnston was a neighborhood friend of mine and a senior; Martin Despins was the only person ever to have been drummed out of "The

Black Thirteen"; Paul was our homeroom's "...man of distinction who makes himself heard...a humorist and salesman who enjoys Wagner...plans to go to Teacher's College to learn to educate future scholars in general science and skulduggery."

David, whom I barely remember, was a senior, "...friendly and ambitious...Art Editor of *The* [1951] *Annual*...a hard worker with a determined spirit...has real artistic talent...a biology student...a go-getter...intends to be a science teacher." Arthur Von Au was "...the popular co-editor of this book," *The Annual* for 1952, "a Herculean job which he filled adequately...is an accomplished dancer and an artist of the keyboard...President of the German Club...'Art' intends to go to college and is sure to make good." He became a Lutheran minister.

Ray was "Quiet...somewhat introspective...hobbies center about camping, chess playing, philosophy, science fiction...member of Rifle, Chemistry, Biology, and Physics Clubs...pet peeve: French idioms! ...future plans: University of Connecticut, then a teaching career." Actually, he joined the Navy with me, then attended Cornell for a while, City University of New York for many years to finish his degree while he worked as a journalist, and finally he became an evangelical minister.

Jack Rule was "...the likable boy who cooks his food over a Bunsen burner and drinks from a test tube...the best chemist of them all...an honor student...'Jack' should make his mark at Wesleyan." He did. He paid for his tuition by commercially breeding angel fish during his high school years, but he became an alcoholic and ended his own life.

Finally, there was Ben Barnes, a senior and "A top ranking student and diplomat...a real booster for the U. N. ...a hard worker and a good leader... elected member of National Honor Society in his Junior year...likes reading, classical music, and opera...plans to attend Colgate University...we consider Ben the man most likely to succeed." He became an Episcopalian minister, the fourth member of The Fantaseers to take religious orders.

The Constitution of the organization was adopted in March of 1950, and our library established in my house — the parsonage of the First Italian Baptist Church on Windsor Avenue — in April, for we were ostensibly to be a science-fiction reading society, not a fraternity, for fraternities were banned by the school. I was elected Book Custodian, one of two club officers, the other being Treasurer. The last amendment of the Constitution said that "There shall be no set number of members, no restrictions," but that was either forgotten or deliberately violated, for we eventually called ourselves "The Black Thirteen" at a later stage and held our membership to that number.

As might have been predicted, our club soon became primarily social rather than literary. Though no dates are attached to the individual items in the Chronology, here are some of the several outstanding events: "Antecedent Action"— I believe that refers to the party where we were conceived; "Begin[n]ing of club"[;] "First meeting of club[;] Entrence [sic] of Burns and [Pierre]," which must refer to their being inducted; "Ripping down of fence[.]" (I don't recall who made these notes, but the spelling is bad and I won't be pedantic about correcting the errors; from here on I'll do it silently.)

The fence referred to was composed of trash — bedsprings, old boards, anything and everything, and it had been erected by a neighbor of mine across the large weed-overgrown vacant lot behind his house. This field had never been turned into a back yard with a lawn, nor even a garden. We used to cut through it to get to a street that dead-ended at the lot, and when the neighbor put up his fence, which was both an eyesore and an offense to us, we had to go a very long way around or climb over it.

I am startled to look over the records now and discover that this episode occurred so early in the history of The Fantaseers; specifically, in the early fall of our first year. It was intended as an initiation ceremony for Marty Despins, a sophomore (though none was required by our Constitution), and we all participated in it. Our great mistake was to split up afterward: half the club retreated to my house, the other half sat in Pierre's car across the street, in front of the Venice Restaurant where a cruising police car, called by our neighbor, stopped, interrogated the passengers, and took down names. Though I wasn't one of those caught, it fell out that, as the club's chief officer, I had to go to the neighbor to apologize and to make restitution for the fence. I believe the sum came to something like $10.00, and I assume we all contributed.

Johnston was the first and only member of The Fantaseers to resign, as of October first of 1950. I think his mother made him drop out. In any case, he was a friend of mine, but not of the other members, and not literary in any particular way. The club must have taken out its frustration over the incident of the fence on Marty, whose idea it was, because he is the only member ever to have been ousted. The entry in the club diary read, "RESIGNED, as of November 10, 1950 — by Request **** Martin D———-s, Member." Several members were suspended from time to time for non-payment of the dues with which we purchased science fiction and fantasy books: David, in January of 1951, Arthur in April, Peter, Pierre, Paul, and Lindsey in May, but the suspensions were always lifted. Other items, many of them lost in the dim regions of the Vale of Lethe, read, "Sending of horse crap to Phineas; Breaking of window at Venice; PEARL STREET; Turco's accident with Pierre's car." I remember none of these except the last.

When Pierre's father had established his plant nursery in Kensington the family moved there, but Pierre never broke his ties with his old friends. He was the only Fantaseer not a student at Meriden High. Of course, he had to have a car under the circumstances. Before I had my own, on occasion I went out to practice driving Pierre's dad's stick-shift truck on the dirt roads of the nursery. When I got good enough, Pierre would let me practice with his automobile.

One day we were parked across the street from my house, beside a mail depository. I got behind the wheel and Pierre walked around to get in on the passenger side. Just as Pierre opened his door, my foot slipped off the clutch and the car jerked forward. Pierre jumped out of the way in time to avoid being caught between the door and the mailbox, but the door hit the box and was sprung.

Strictly speaking, this episode had nothing to do with The Fantaseers except that it involved two members, but many of us saw nearly everything we did in terms of the club, or the Sportlanders Barbershop Quartet in which I sang lead, or the Fantatnafs, which is what we called ourselves when we were joined by the Reesatnafs, the girls in our group. Those were certainly my personal parameters; schoolwork almost didn't enter into consideration. Intellectually, I was concerned nearly exclusively with reading and with my own writing. I knew very early what I wanted to be.

That's why I'm embarrassed now to read the misspellings in this list of Fantaseer events, for I've always thought of myself as an excellent speller, and it must have been I who typed this list because I recognize the elite typeface of my father's old Underwood Standard typewriter. How could I forget it? Every week I sat at the keyboard hunting and pecking out stories and poems, many of the latter published in *The Morning Record* in Lydia Atkinson's Wednesday poetry column, "Pennons of Pegasus." If I had spent my writing time on homework I would very likely have been a member of the National Honor Society like a number of The Fantaseers, which did not include Paul or Burns.

The chronology continues: "Flashbulb lighting." A classic Fantaseer event! I had a flashgun that I could set off without the camera. One Friday evening several of us got into Pierre's car and began cruising, a great American teen-age pastime. We motored up to Hubbard Park on the farthest western edge of town and drove around Mirror Lake slowly, peering into the windows of the automobiles parked there. When we at last found a couple making out in the back seat we cruised slowly past, I leaned out the window and set off the flashgun, and Pierre floored the accelerator. We got to West Main Street quickly, but there was so much traffic that, by the time we entered the stream, our victim's car was right behind us.

We beat about country roads for a while, but we couldn't shake our pursuer, so we changed our strategy. "Head for downtown!" Burns yelled. On Friday evenings the stores stayed open late and when we got to the business district we began doing circles around Crown Street Square until we got stopped at a light, the furious lover right behind us, revving his engine. It happened that we'd pulled up next to another high schooler's jalopy on our right, so I leaned from the window again and yelled to the driver Don Wescott, "How about cutting off that guy?" I pointed with my thumb. "He's chasing us."

Don immediately put his car into reverse, stuck his left rear fender and bumper in between our pursuer and us, turned off his engine, pulled the keys from the ignition, threw them on the floor and began hunting for them. The light turned green and we were off in a blare of horns and curses.

The fellow who'd been chasing us had taken down Pierre's license number and evidently gotten his home address from the motor vehicles bureau. He called and, when Pierre answered and identified himself, asked, "How much do you want for the negatives?" Pierre had a hard time explaining that there were no negatives because we had no camera, only a flashgun. "I don't think he really believed me," Pierre told us. We all wondered who he was and with whom he'd been out that night.

"Fixing muffler at hunting lodge; Play rehearsals"— this referred to the Salem Witch Trials playlet I wrote for The Fantaseers to enact during the annual Senior Skit Day at the high school. "Robes at First Congo; Burning alcohol in Congo basement"— good grief! I don't remember that at all. "Priest act in Kensington."

Another classic.

The Fantaseers needed black choir robes for the play, and we could have borrowed them from my father's, or from George's father's church. We chose the latter, and while we had them we decided to put them to double employ. Out near Pierre's nursery one of the roads where I had learned to drive was used, like the Mirror Lake road, as a lover's lane. One evening The Fantaseers went out, parked some distance away, cut through the woods where, before emerging, we put on the robes and formed a wedge behind Paul, who was the guidon-bearer. He carried a crucifix made of crooked sticks. Ben came next, portly and archiepiscopal, the only one of us wearing a surplice. Flanking him a step behind came Burns to the left and I to the right, bearing lighted candles. The rest fanned out behind with prayerful hands upraised.

We walked into the middle of the road and began marching down it. Paul intoned, "Repent ye, sinners, and be saved!" Ben waved his blessings over the automobiles with their stunned occupants. Burns lifted his candle and made the sign of the cross over the lovers in their autos, I sang "Jesus Loves Me." The tapers flickered in the summer zephyrs, everyone chanted or called out to the sinners lining both sides of the dirt track — we raised a glorious and cacophonic din unto the Lord.

As the phalanx approached two cars on either flank the headlights blinked on, the engines croaked to life, and, wheels spinning, the vehicles roared off into the night. It was as though we were starting a serial drag race. Soon there were no cars left on Lovers' Lane, and the Fantaseers glowed with good feeling. "Just think how many souls we've saved tonight," Burns said with that Irish grin sitting under his nose. "At least temporarily."

The next entry is "THE PLAY," of which I have a photo taken by a senior, Howard Iwanicki, who became a photographer for *The Morning Record*. Ben is seated in the makeshift judge's bench, laughing insanely as he snips the heads off a string of paper dolls. He has on one of the black choir robes, as does Arthur who is standing beside him to his right as an officer of the court, I suppose, holding one of those long-handled window poles they used to have in the old school buildings. Both of them are wearing new mop heads as wigs.

Burns is the witch, evidently. He is sitting, dressed in rags and chains, his chin in his left hand and his elbow on his knee. Behind him, dressed entirely in black and looking like a flat silhouette, stands Jack, the headsman. Paul lurks to his left, also in rags, gotten up as a hunchback with a crooked walking stick. I'm next, sitting down, in my father's old swallow-tail coat and raggedy white pants. Peter and George are next, in the jury box, the latter dressed in what appears to be a white sheet.

The chronology of Fantaseer events continues. "Jacklighting at the Tower" had to do with the spotlight my mother had won at CUNO Engineering Corp. where she was a stenographer for years during and after the war. As my parents never owned a car, she had stuck it in the bottom of a trunk. I'd asked her for permission to attach it to my first jalopy, a 1940 Chevrolet tudor sedan, but she had refused me, which I felt was unreasonable as she had no earthly use for it herself. So I expropriated it. I disguised it by putting a tennis racquet cover over it, and she didn't notice it for months.

I don't know what it was we were jacklighting — certainly not animals. The "tower" was Castle Craig on East Peak, a lookout above Hubbard Park that had been privately built by an eccentric man and then either donated or bequeathed to the city. We used to drive up there all the time for rituals and romance. One Christmas Eve Ray and I and Tony, the tenor in the Sportlanders Quartet, tried to drive up to East Peak. We had been sneaking home-made wine from Tony's father's cellar, so it wasn't till we got half way up the twisting climb that we realized we were driving on glare ice. We had at last noticed because the car had stopped and was beginning to drift backward, despite the fact that its wheels were still spinning. I stopped, put on the emergency brake, and stepped out of the car to assess the situation. My feet skidded out from under me and I fell flat on my back in the middle of the road. I was stone sober in an instant.

Somehow we managed to get the car turned around and headed downhill again, but I couldn't control it and we hit the guard rail, denting the fender so badly it scraped the tire. We pulled the metal away from the rubber and, after heroic labors, managed to reach the city streets around midnight. Both Tony and Ray were Catholics, but we knew that George's father was conducting a service at that hour, so we drove downtown, parked, and staggered down the middle aisle to the only pew that was unoccupied, way down in front. I thought we'd pulled it off, but in fact everyone knew we were drunk, it turned out. Jean, my future wife, was in the congregation with her family that night. When we talk about it these days she still gets that look on her face.

Another entry reads, "Burns works at Kresge's" with Curt and me. The three of us were stockboys at the five-and-dime, as I recall, unless I was still a busboy at the snack bar. Not much later in the chronicle there is an entry that reads, "Burns works at Palace," that is, the Palace Theatre on West Main, a few blocks up from Kresge's. Burns was always a slow mover, though he would have preferred to call his actions "deliberate," I'm sure. He must not have lasted long as a stock boy, but he looked like the archetypal usher with his round, flat hat, red uniform, flashlight and freckles. He made a ceremony of it when any of The Fantaseers showed up for a show.

Here's an interesting item: "Bev naked on bed." Why don't I remember Bev? Perhaps I wasn't present. Burns, when I began this past summer to reminisce about one of our adventures, said, "I wasn't in on that one." And so not all of our "common memories" are common. A fond recollection turns into something other than the warm sharing of remembrance. Suddenly, there's a blank place where we thought someone was standing. Here's one I don't recall: "Burns in Hubbard Park fixing motor in rain assailed by six-foot bruiser."

A major item — I shall reproduce it exactly: "Ben mispells Fantaseers on Jubalee Program." That's worth the whole list, it seems to me. "Ben pushes Burns into ten feet of water," and Burns couldn't swim. "Burns meets Tut on way home from Hubbard Park"— Tut was no doubt the "bruiser" who had accosted Burns earlier. He was tall, not big, but scary enough for all that — one of the town bullies, of no particular occupation and a small-time gang reputation.

"Ben's car [gasoline indicator] needle stuck: 2:00 [a.m.] in Kensington. My mother won't speak to me for 9 months." And little wonder at that. "Pierre's party in Sept.: Paul hanging from rafters. Sugar in Turco's gas tank," and a new carburetor for Turco. "Graduation party: Class of '51." The ranks of the Fantaseers were considerably depleted by the end of the summer. We lost Burns, George, Dave, Ben, and, of course, Lindsey to Yale a year early. "Burns has chance to go to Arabia; Trip to see 'King Lear'; Holding court in room 8; Burns and Peter playing cards in auditorium till school closes; Burns works in Beanfields; Until the sea shall give up its treasures. Hot Dog Roast in Burns' yard; Mrs. Turco's opinion of Paul and Burns; Burns, Paul and Ben go to shack in woods; Burns changes site of Meriden Library." That one is a real puzzler.

"Fantaseers and Reesatnafs go on midnight hike to tower"— Castle Craig again. "Locking Burns and George in safe...Burns and Paul make Peter eat Pizza until he spews; Trying to teach Ben to cut out paper dolls; Trying to teach Burns to snap his fingers...." Obviously, this list isn't in chronological order after all, since the play was over and there would be no reason at this point to teach Ben the art of paper-doll manufacture.

No such list exists for our senior year, but the incident that Burns didn't remember in 1991 was the quintessential Fantaseers terrorist action. The reason he wasn't involved, I now realize, is that he had graduated and gone his way. When the Class of 1951 had disappeared into the mists, those Fantaseers who remained inducted new members including a replacement George, as I recall. One good-natured but not very bright sophomore, Bobby, wanted very much to join, and he began hanging around with us. He became a sort of mascot, but he had no interest in reading, just in deviltry, so he was never made a member.

Bobby fed us the information that there was a car that parked every Wednesday night on a deserted stretch of road out by Black Pond on the East Side near where he lived. He had followed the occupant, a man, who cut through some woods to visit a house whose occupants were two young women. He would stay for a time, come out, walk through the woods back to his car, get in, and drive off. We were intrigued. Our outraged "moral" sense was activated, as it had been in the lover's lane incidents.

I worked for the *Record* in my senior year, and one of my jobs was to pick up "mats" at the railroad station each night. I got to know the railroad men, and when the Fantaseers' plan began to jell, I asked for and obtained a railroad flare. I thought I knew how to start it by scraping its head on a hard surface, like a Lucifer match.

One night the Fantaseers went up to Black Pond and most of the club members hid behind a stone wall that flanked the spot where the car was parked. I hid my car up the road, and Ray and I got ready to go into action when we got the flashlight signal from the others. When the light flashed, that meant that the owner of the car had come back and was about to start his engine. I was to plant the lighted flare in the middle of the road to stop him. What happened after that was to be played by ear, I guess. Ray was my lookout, but he never warned me because he never got a signal. I heard the car coming, dashed out into the road, squatted, began madly rubbing the flare against the macadam, and jumped out of the way just as the automobile came roaring past. I was angry and derisive of my colleagues in terror, who had remained hidden behind the wall. They resolved to do better next time.

Paul, borrowing a leaf from the lover who had chased us down from Hubbard Park to Crown Street Square the year before, called the Connecticut Motor Vehicles Department. He said that a car with such-and-such a license plate number was parking on private property, and he wanted to get a name and address to inform the offender he'd best park elsewhere. Then he went to the Meriden City Hall Clerk's office to find the names of the women living in the house in the woods. Paul assembled a considerable dossier on the principals. He found that the man was married and lived in Plainville, an adjoining town. Paul even scouted the neighborhood.

This time there was to be no flare. We all hid behind the wall, I with my trusty flashgun, Paul with a flashlight and his dossier, the rest with their courage screwed up. The plan was that we'd all rise, holler and make lots of light and noise, and hightail it off across the pastures. To make sure the parker had some trouble roaring down the road as he'd done last time, we let half the air out of his tires, and Paul pulled his old sugar-in-the-gas-tank trick.

But the boys were out to prove their manhood. When our victim arrived, we rose up as a body from behind the stone fence. Paul called out in stentorian tones, "John Doe, 2121 Adams Drive, Plainville, Connecticut!" The man stopped in his tracks, his hand on the car door. My flashgun fired. Following the plan, Ray and I headed off across the field. When my flight was arrested by an electric fence I grabbed in the dark with my bare hand, I cursed, turned, and saw in the moonlight a row of Fantaseers standing at the low wall. Paul was still unreeling his list of facts. The man was immobile. I began to walk back, but before I arrived he jumped into his car and took off...as best he could.

We were in no great hurry. We strolled in a leisurely manner to my hidden car, got in, and followed the fleeing vehicle — down East Main to Broad Street, where we decided to peel off and go to Plainville by a back route. It was as though it were planned: as the man pulled into his home street, we pulled out of the next street up and fell in right behind him again. My spotlight was on, and we played it over his car. He pulled into his driveway, jumped out of the car, and ran inside. He lived on a little circle, and we cruised around it hooting at him, shining the light on the front of his house, and then we slowly pulled away. As we did so, we noticed a police car driving past us. Before we turned the corner, we saw it stop in front of our victim's house. Bobby said he never saw the man again.

There were other escapades after that, as for instance when we tried to make a huge torch out of Castle Craig by soaking its stone-and-steel construction with kerosene, but the Adventure of the Black Pond Parker was both the crest and the trough of our careers as Fantaseers. When he graduated, Bobby joined the service, I heard, and when he was discharged he and another young veteran held up a gasoline station and fled across the state line where they ran out of money and held up another place. They were caught, tried as second offenders, even though they'd not been convicted of the first offense, and were sentenced to some incredibly long incarceration for armed robbery — if my memory serves, it was life, and when they'd served their minimum sentences, they were to be extradited and tried for the first crime.

"But I never ran into anybody," Burns said, because for years I worked the second shift. When I was awake, everybody else was sleeping, and when I was asleep, everyone else was awake." He'd heard about Paul's death, but had not run into him. He'd heard about Jack's alcoholism, the loss of his job and his family, his suicide.

Burns hadn't known about Peter's exceedingly successful appearances on "The Price is Right" and "The Wheel of Fortune" before he was divorced a second time, could no longer find a job, and was reduced to asking for long-distance collect-call handouts from his friends.

"We'll have to get together again next year," Burns said.

"We've got a lot to catch up on."

Just as he was leaving Jean came in from shopping. I introduced them. "Do you remember me?" he asked, giving her his patented Irish grin. She assured him she did. "I'd like you both to meet my wife," Burns said. "She went to Meriden High, too, a few years behind us. She's real tall."

"We're looking forward to it," I said, shaking his hand. We waved to each other as he drove away down the hot August streets of Oswego.

Lewis Turco's '40 Chevy jalopy in the driveway of the parsonage of the First Italian Baptist Church

PIERRE OF SUNNY BORDER

It was a Halloween party at Pierre's home in Kensington in the fall of 1950 that gave me the material for my first great literary success. I had gotten to know Pierre when he and his family lived on South Vine Street in Meriden, Connecticut. He attended Meriden High School during our sophomore year, 1949-50, but even then his father owned the Sunny Border Nursery a few miles down the Chamberlain Highway, which is where Pierre and his family moved before our junior year.

During the intervening summer, however, I got to know the nursery well, for I sometimes worked there with Pierre and Bent, a narrow immigrant Dane who was one of two or three full-time employees. I recall Bent as a simple, silent man whose unvarying lunch, on those steaming hot days in the barn and the fields, was a Hershey Bar sandwich.

Pierre's father was a Dane as well, but his mother was a full-blooded French woman. I liked them both. The father struck me as being the epitome of Danishness: slender, not talkative, but not unapproachable, either. He had blue eyes and light brown hair; he was intelligent and efficient. The mother, on the other hand, was sweet and excitable. She spoke in a rapid, heavily-accented English, and she seemed always in a flutter over something or other.

Lillian, Pierre's sister, was two or three years older than we and she was ravishingly beautiful, I thought. She turned me into a bashful and awkward preadolescent whenever she appeared, a feature of her presence that filled me with chagrin.

Pierre and I used to go out into the dark fields in the simmering evenings and play juvenile games like hide-and-seek. Another thing we liked to do was to sneak up on the cars of petting teenagers parked along the dirt road that skirted the nursery. One dark night we slunk through the fringe of woods to within a few yards of such a car, close enough to eavesdrop on the conversation of the couple who occupied the front seat. The girl was saying, "What are you doing? Leave my buttons alone. Stop it!"

The boy replied, "Button, button, who's got the button?"

She kept protesting, but not very seriously, and he kept repeating his phrase until Pierre and I could stand it no more. My hand was resting on a large stone, so I lifted it, arose, heaved it and shouted, "Button, button, who's got the friggin' button?" The stone went crashing through the trees and so did Pierre and I, in the opposite direction, snirtling and giggling.

I was to turn sixteen on the second of May of 1950, and I had determined to buy a car, a 1940 Chevrolet, from one of my older co-workers at Kresge's Five and Ten Cent Store, where I had spent part of the school year as busboy at the fountain. I had been saving my money, and, in order to eke out these sums to reach the $350.00 I needed, I had decided to sell my tropical fish and equipment which stood on tables in the sunporch of the parsonage where we lived.

I shared the room with my father, who had a private sanctum behind some bookcases there. I would sometimes spend an evening dreaming into the murky light seeping out of the thick glass of a tank full of angel fish or gouramis, the night outdoors lapping at the windows like dark water. To passers-by perhaps I looked like an aquarian myself. I could hear my father nearby working on the sermons he would deliver on Sunday in the pulpit of the white-clapboarded First Italian Baptist

Church that stood next door. A green, glass-shaded lamp on one of the bookcases dropped its liquid glow onto his head and mine, though we couldn't see each other. The light seemed filtered through decaying vegetation. Later, when I left home, I would dream of that room.

In the dream I would be seated before the aquaria. It would be night. The fish would be swimming in their dark waters, and as I watched, they would swim up into the air of the room and maneuver about me. There was no boundary between surface and fathom. I would look into the largest aquarium, trace the leaves of the rust-colored sword plant to its root, and there I would see my father's skull half-buried in the gravel, the stalk of the plant growing out of his socket. It wasn't a pleasant dream, nor was it a nightmare. The emotions I felt were those of nostalgia and ruefulness, of some sort of vague longing and regret. Still, I didn't enjoy the dream's recurrence, and at last I exorcised it unwittingly by writing a poem about it.

To prepare for my purchasing the car Pierre would sometimes let me practice driving the stick-shift truck that belonged to the nursery. I remember our sitting on the front seat the first time, Pierre beside me, and his telling me, "Now, shift into low, and let out the clutch at the same time that you press down on the accelerator." The resulting series of lurches and bumps tossed the truck along the dirt road and our bodies into the air of the cab and from side to side.

"Slow! Slow! Let it out slow!" Pierre yelled, gasping. At last we came to rest. Eventually, after many hazards were passed, I learned how to shift.

My birthday came; Curt Offen let me borrow his mother's car to take the road test in — I don't recall why the Chevy wasn't available that day. Curt's car was a '46 Ford with lots more oomph than mine had. The moment I slid in to take the examination was actually the first time I'd been behind the car's wheel, and its responses were so much greater than expected that I had to apologize to the driving inspector and explain why I was roaring backward into my parallel-parking slot and burning rubber when I took off. To my amazement, and to Curt's, I passed the test on first try. That same week I bought the Chevy, the only automobile my family had while I lived at home, and I was born into freedom even though the engine burned nearly as much oil as it did gas.

It must have been that same summer of 1950 when Pierre and his family moved permanently out to Kensington from Meriden, but that didn't sever the ties he had with his friends. By no means. He was around almost as much after the move as he had been before it, for he owned a car as well. There were many, many days when I traveled to Kensington, alone or with a load of Fantaseers; or Pierre, who was one of the original Fantaseers, came to Meriden. It was the Fantatnafs — the Fantaseers plus the Reesatnafs, our women's auxiliary — who filled the Sunny Border Nurseries barn that fateful Halloween.

Paul hung on the rafters and made noises like a monkey while he scratched under his arms. I tasted black coffee with sugar for the first time that night, drinking it with fresh doughnuts made by Pierre's mother, and became an addict. We sang songs and bobbed for apples, swilled cider, played games, ate candy, and raised Hob.

Halloween was on a Tuesday that year, so the next day was a school day. I spent it writhing in bed, however, for I had the most tremendous bellyache. "You ate too much candy last night," my mother said. "Let me give you an enema." It was her standard cure for stomach troubles.

"It's not an ordinary stomach ache," I said. "Please, take me to the doctor." It was an amazing thing for me to request, but for some reason she'd have no part of it. I'd just overeaten.

On the other hand, I'd have no part of an enema. By mid-afternoon my father was beginning to think that perhaps I had something more than merely a gut gripe after all. At last he helped me out to a taxi. I was nearly doubled in half.

When the doctor saw me he prodded me a bit on the right side and I groaned in anguish. He looked at my father and said, "Acute appendicitis. He'll have to be operated on immediately." I can recollect the look of astonishment and anger — at my mother, probably — in Daddy's eyes. And so I was rushed off to the hospital.

When I came out of the anesthetic I was sicker than when I'd gone under it. I vomited green bile, and with every heave my new stitches strained and an agony of excruciating pain bloomed in my abdomen, but at last things calmed down and I no longer wished to die.

In those days one had to remain in hospital for a week after an appendectomy, and one wasn't allowed to walk for two or three days, so I was given a wheelchair. At once I was a traffic menace to my floor. I sailed down the halls at a great rate, turning in and out of doors, around corners, visiting everyone, nearly knocking a doctor down on one occasion, but he stepped aside at the last moment as I rounded a bend and cried, "Whoa! Sorry." No one seemed to get angry with me, though. I don't even recall a reprimand from the doctor. I asked all the young nurses to marry me.

My chastened mother came to visit every day with my rueful father. The Fantaseers and the Reesatnafs came to see me after school. And eventually I was allowed to go home. When I got back to class I discovered that Doc Michele, our junior-year English teacher, had given the class an assignment to write an essay on a personal experience. I had plenty of material, so I sat down at my father's old Underwood Standard typewriter in the sunporch behind the bookcases, and I hunted-and-pecked off a piece I titled "Appendix Excitis."

Life went on. I commissioned Pierre, an artist whose medium, in those days, was oils, to paint me a scene of horror, the details of which I specified, for I was nothing if not addicted to tales of terror and the supernatural as well as science fiction. I recall that one feature of the painting was a disgusting pool of slime out of which a clawed arm was reaching toward the corpse of a hanged man that dangled above the tarn. I hung it on the wall of my bedroom and was thoroughly delighted with it. My mother hated it and threatened all kinds of destruction, which I didn't take seriously. She wouldn't dare touch anything of mine.

At least, she wouldn't while I was at home. But time passed and I graduated from high school. Pierre did as well, from Kensington High, and he attended Princeton where he became an English major which surprised me, for I thought he had some talent as an artist. I am writing this in September of 1991, and yesterday I had a request from a publisher to send some family photographs to use as illustrations in a forthcoming collection of my poems titled *Murmurs in the Walls*. I found one picture, from the early 1960s, not that I wanted to send but to contemplate. It is of my dear old friend and mentor, the late Loring Williams. He is sitting on a couch in our apartment in Cleveland. My two-year-old daughter Melora is standing next to him on the couch. Her mouth is open — she is talking around her pacifier. Overhead, hanging on the wall, I notice today, are two pictures. One is a stylized picture of "Blue Dogs" by Tony, the Sportlanders' tenor, who went to Pratt institute and became an advertising executive. The other is a roofscape in sunlit white by Pierre. I haven't seen that picture in years, but I'm sure we still have it hidden away somewhere, and I still like it.

One day a decade or so earlier I had come back from the Navy on leave or liberty, and I noticed that Pierre's depiction of the hanging man was missing from its wonted space on my wall. I asked my mother what had happened to it, and she replied that she'd carried out her threat and thrown it away. At first I couldn't believe she'd done so, and I searched through the house, but I never found it. I know it was a stupid painting, but I would like to have it, and I never forgave my mother for the only act of censorship she ever carried out against her son's taste in art or literature.

Pierre worked for several years in New York and then, when his father died, he came back to Connecticut and took over the nursery. Jean and I seldom get back to Meriden anymore, but one of those times many years ago I heard from my brother Gene who, five years later, followed my tracks into the hallowed halls of Meriden High, that for years Doc Michele read "Appendix Excitis" to her English classes. It was, I understand, the only essay by a former student that she ever read to any of them. She never told me she was doing it, but I must say I couldn't have been more pleased when I heard what she'd been up to, for I respected her immensely. I wish I still owned a copy of that ancient paper, but I must not have made a carbon as I usually did. I'd really like to see what all the excitement was about. And I wish I still had Pierre's genre painting.

The Fantaseers' Library, 1951

RAY

Ray and I, like the other young men and women in our high school crowd, had been accepted as college freshmen for the coming fall semester, but there was a difference: Ray and I couldn't afford to go. His father ran a diner on Pratt Street in Meriden, and mine didn't make enough on his preacher's salary to keep the family afloat, for my mother had to work as a stenographer at the Cuno Corp. to make ends meet. It was a surprise to our friends when Ray and I, just before our graduation from Meriden High, signed up to do four years in the Navy. It was a relief to our parents, though, I'm sure.

Our enlistment was a logical move for Ray and me. The Korean War was still on, and if we weren't in college we were draft bait. I think the Fantaseers wrote us off as college material when they heard what we'd done, and perhaps the Reesatnafs did as well. But Ray and I had as our second reason for enlisting the fact that, after we had honorably served our hitches, we would qualify for the G. I. Bill, which would pay our way through college.

We had not, to be accurate, originally intended to join the Navy. We drove down to New Haven one warm June day to join the Coast Guard, by far the safest of the services. We went into our favorite tobacco shops and bookstores just off the New Haven common and on the Yale campus, then we went wandering in confusion around the Post Office and the Federal Office Building looking for a recruiting station. Finally, we approached a policeman on the street and asked him where it was. He informed us that the nearest Coast Guard station was in New London, not New Haven, about sixty miles up Route One. Ray and I, out of sheer laziness, perhaps, or because we detected the hand of Fate in our lives, decided we'd look in on the Navy close at hand.

We discovered, in talking to the recruiting chief, that if we signed on with the Navy we would be guaranteed service schools as "High School Seaman Apprentices." We would even have a choice of general areas in which to be trained after we'd taken some aptitude tests. And so we joined. We went home and told our parents first. I was hurt by the equanimity with which my father took the news — logic is all very good and well, but on some occasions one likes a display of emotion leavened, perhaps, with a dash of misgiving.

Ray lived on Pleasant Street, almost across from the high school, which was built on a steep hill. In our sophomore year, not long after I had learned to drive, gotten my license, and bought my first car from my savings and the sale of my many tropical fish and aquaria, I was supposed to meet the Fantaseers out in front of Ray's one evening. I drove into the private driveway next to the school in order to back out and turn around, but the driveway rolled precipitously downhill, and I sat there with my foot on the brake thinking, What happens if I stall and the emergency brake doesn't hold?

Across the street, where I couldn't see them, the fellows were standing on Ray's porch. Ray asked, "Is that Turk?" Lore recounts Paul's answer — "If he backs out and hits that silver Mercury in front of your house, it's Turk."

I sat in the front seat of my '40 Chevy sweating. Finally, I shifted into reverse, pulled my foot off the brake, hit the accelerator, and quickly let up on the clutch. The car burned rubber for a heartbeat, then roared backwards up the drive, hurtled across the street, and destroyed the left side of the Merc. I got out of the car to survey the damage but never heard the strangled laughter of the Fantaseers on the porch. I learned then that there is little compassion in the world, for one of the most terrifying moments of my adolescent life provided my "friends" with humor for years, and no doubt still provides it when those who are left remember.

There is a picture in our 1952 yearbook *The Annual*—which I co-edited with Art von Au — of Ray and me sitting in our English honors classroom beside the window, staring out at the hedge that separated the High School from that driveway. Though the picture was staged, the pose was nevertheless typical. The title of my entry that year in the Hicks Prize Essay Contest — it was one of the six finalists — was "A Row of Hedges," and it made an elaborate metaphor: the hedges represented the succession of our school years; the window cut off the view of the downhill end of the hedges, which represented the future, etc., etc. Quite corny, but decently written for a high school senior, evidently.

In the same *Annual* is the equally corny class ode, "Graduation," which Ray and I wrote in collaboration — he did a "free verse" (i.e., prose) original draft and I cast it into iambic pentameter blank verse. Peter said to me years after we'd left Meriden that he would never forgive me if he somehow discovered that Ray and I had meant it as a joke. I remember considering, given my relationship with Ray, that such an intent had been a distinct possibility, but I'd never thought of it till Peter brought it up. Perhaps he was remembering another irreverent ode on which Ray and I had collaborated earlier, to the World War II correspondent Ernie Pyle. Written in Hunky Doran's physics class, it read something like this — I quote from treacherous memory:

> Pyle's laid low.
> Ernie's piled.
> Pyle's laid low in the pile
> Where everyone's Pyled
> Eventually.

On the morning at the end of the first week in July after graduation, when Ray and I were to travel to the recruiting station in New York City, Ray missed the train at the Meriden depot. He was technically A. W. O. L. to begin his enlistment, but he managed to catch up with me in New York — his father drove him to New Haven where he caught other transportation down. It's interesting to look back and see that both his behavior on that occasion and mine would typify our Naval careers. Instead of waiting for him, I followed orders and got on the train, but it was missing ship's movement several years later that would get Ray into deep trouble. Depending on one's viewpoint, my actions were either disloyal or exemplary; his were either romantic or irresponsible.

No need to chronicle our early Navy careers in detail. Both Ray and I intended to be writers one day — we'd worked together in our Senior year for our home town paper, *The Morning Record* — but his tests showed an aptitude for electronics and mine were all clerical. I became a yeoman striker — I've always been bemused by that term for a clerk; what "a farmer who cultivates his own land" has to do with naval paper pushing is mystifying. Ray went on to Fire Control school — another misleading designation. He was not to become a fireman, but a technician who serviced the radar installations that controlled gunnery. Both schools were located at Bainbridge Naval Training Center in Maryland. After we had completed boot camp I went to school for six weeks to learn to type and file. Ray's training lasted nearly a year, however, so he stayed on in Bainbridge while I went to the Naval Air Technical Training Center at Norman, Oklahoma.

I hated the place. The only thing I liked about it was my pet horned toad, which I carried around with me in my jumper pocket and eventually sent back east to Paul who was attending New Britain State Teachers' College.

While I was still in boot camp I'd applied for the NROTC program. If I were selected, I would be released from active duty to attend college, after which I would return to the Navy as an officer. I was informed, after only three months in the empty prairie, that I had indeed been chosen to attend an intensive, six-week high school refresher back at Bainbridge and, incidentally, to rejoin Ray.

When I got there I met a Marine who had, like me, been accepted at Tufts University as a journalism major. If we passed the Prep School and were selected by a board, we would go there, take our B. A.'s, and then come back into the Navy to finish our tours of duty as officers.

There were tests at the end of each two-week segment. I got good scores on the first set of tests, but my Marine friend flunked them by scores so low that, no matter how well he did on the next two sets, he could not achieve a passing grade. The same thing happened to both of us on the second and third tries — he failed, I passed. So we both waited for the list of those who had been selected for the school to be posted, I with concern, but he with no hope at all.

At last the moment came, and we went to see if our names were included. His name was on the list; mine was not! I asked the commandant of the school how this could be. "True, you passed the tests and he failed," the C.O. told me, "but he had a good high school record and you didn't, and his scores were improving while yours were sliding. We thought he'd be a better risk." This, of course, was specious logic. A more likely reason would be that my name ended in a vowel and the marine's did not; nevertheless, he went to Medford, and I went to sea.

On the evening of the day I was notified of my failure, Ray and I went into Washington, D. C., to get drunk. When we returned to base (barely!) I spent a while waiting to be assigned to the fleet, and Ray went back to school. The Bureau of Naval Personnel eventually sent me to Brooklyn Naval Shipyard to help commission the new version of the U.

S. S. Hornet, a carrier, and after that we had sea trials in the Caribbean, then a world cruise to the far east through the Panama Canal. For my last year I was assigned to BuPers in Arlington, Virginia — I'd come, literally, full circle in my four years. Eventually Ray, too, was assigned carrier duty, but not aboard the *Hornet*.

During those final three years of our hitches, Ray and I managed to see one another from time to time, and on one of our liberties I met his girlfriend, Randy, who was a student at Pratt Institute in Brooklyn. I liked her a great deal, and I thought Ray ought to cultivate his relationship with her. He did, but she was the cause of his missing ship's movement. The story, in the straight 1950s, was startling at best, though such things are more commonplace nowadays: Randy had decided she was not heterosexually inclined. She took up residence with another young woman; they had a spat, and Randy's friend out of spite went out and picked up a sailor who got her pregnant. The women reconciled their differences, and they decided to raise the baby together — it turned out to be a male child. Ray got himself wound up in this situation, and in one of his efforts to help Randy disentangle her life, he missed his ship.

Romantic behavior again, to say the least.

Meanwhile, he and I had begun testing a literary theory we had discussed in high school; namely, that the way to begin a literary career was either to start small by submitting one's early work to the little magazines (my view), or to wait until one had developed a fair level of skill and then begin publishing immediately in the best-known literary periodicals (Ray's stance). In 1953, a year out of high school, one year into the Navy, I began publishing poems in the quarterlies. Ray managed to jar me out in Oklahoma by sending me a story he said he'd published in a well-known science fiction magazine under a pseudonym. The pseudonym was plausible, I bought it, and he had his laugh. But by the time we were discharged, I had a respectable publication record to take to college and graduate school with my new wife, Jean, in 1956, and Ray had nothing in print.

Ray managed to attend a year or so of Cornell on the G. I. Bill. Before he finished, though, he dropped out and took to selling peanuts in the subways of New York City. One day, while he was taking a break from hawking his goobers, he picked up a copy of *The New York Times* to check the classified ads and saw a request for people who could write, which he answered and converted into a job for the Dow-Jones Publishing Co. He eventually became an editor for them, though he had no degree and was, in fact, still taking night school courses at City College.

And he met his lady-love, an elderly widow at least twenty years older than he, with two nearly-grown children. Ray married her and put aside his aspirations for a degree in order to get the kids, brother and sister, through college first. The damned guy was being magnanimous and romantic again — it set my teeth on edge. Here I was, supposed to be the poet, and there he was, the Dow-Jones editor, acting like the poet. I always thought he had married this ancient lass in order to avoid the uncertainties of loving a younger woman who might come replete with such complications as those he had run into with Randy.

When, eventually, his step-children were seen safely through college and Ray himself had gotten his B. A. at long last, and when he had become a youngish widower, I gave a poetry reading at Dr. Generosity's in New York City. Ray came to hear me with one of the two young women he was seeing and trying to decide between. The one he brought with him that night was wonderful, I thought: attractive, lively, mature in a used-but-not-overused way that gave some interesting character lines to her face. She had a young child. The other woman had been his cross-street neighbor in New Jersey where he and his first wife had moved from their oft-burglarized penthouse in the City in order to overlook the lonely coast — I saw pictures of her. She was blonde,

Nordic, no doubt better looking than her rival, but somehow, I felt, the wrong choice, from everything Ray had told me about her.

Of course, it was the blonde Ray chose. He came to Oswego for a visit before he married her. He said he'd quit his job at Dow-Jones, bought a camper, and was taking some time off before he decided what to do with the rest of his life. He wanted somehow to pursue that old dream of ours and see if he couldn't turn into the creative writer he'd never had time to become. After he left, we continued to exchange Christmas cards for a while, and then he disappeared with his new wife.

It was a fluke that got us back in touch with one another. His sister in Connecticut — I had taken her out on one date when we were young — saw something of mine published somewhere and wrote to ask if I'd heard anything of Ray. When I replied, no, I hadn't, she sent me his new address in California. I put him back on our Christmas card list but didn't try to get in closer touch with him. When Jean and I got cards in return we noticed that they were really from his wife (he finally had children of his own by that time), who was evidently a religious enthusiast of an ordinary variety: she stuck little inspirational printed notes in with the seasonal messages. I must admit that such behavior tended to distance me; I remembered all that fatuous nonsense from my days as a preacher's kid.

Then, one day, Ray phoned. "What are you up to?" I asked him. It turned out that he was working for a newspaper in California.

"I've been doing a series on a corruption trial," he said, "and I want to turn it into a book. I need the names of agents. Can you send me some?"

"Sure," I said. "What else is new?"

"Well, I'm quitting this job once the book is done and I'm going to go to a religious camp for a year or so and become a preacher."

At my end there was a stunned silence as I recalled Ray's Roman Catholic upbringing on Polish Hill in Meriden, at St. Stanislaus' church

Fantaseers

a block away from the high school; as I remembered the flippant irreligiosity of The Fantaseers — which, now that I thought of it, had harbored two ministers' sons and produced three other ministers in later life: Art von Au, the Lutheran; George Hangen, a Congregationalist, and Ben Barnes, an Episcopalian. And now a revivalist, evidently. I recall giving a short, incredulous laugh and saying, "What brought this on?" As though I didn't know.

"The Lord told me to do it." Which was not the answer I'd surmised.

"The Lord? How does he go about it? I'd really like to know."

"He just does," Ray said. "If you fight it, He makes sure you regret it. When He wants you to do something, you have to do it. This is something I have to do."

When we hung up I thought, No doubt, no doubt. But I'd be surprised if your wife didn't have more to do with it than the Lord.

Then Ray disappeared again for a while and, three or four years later, resurfaced in Ohio where he was attending some sort of seminary. One day in the mail there appeared a request for money. Ray had been invited to go to China to do missionary work. He was selling what he had left to sell because, although the missionary society would pay his way, he had to foot the fare and the upkeep of his family. I'm afraid I failed to respond. The Chinese, I felt, had their own ways to find salvation.

A bit later, another request. Again I didn't respond, and then a final letter: the offer to travel to China had been withdrawn because, after Tienanmen Square, the government of The People's Republic had closed its gates against Enthusiasts from the West.

And that was the end of it for quite a while. I heard nothing more of Ray, his book, his mission. Jean and I received no more Christmas cards from California, land of fashions, sunshine, and blondness, nor from the overseas dominions of Mao and the Lord. I suppose I should stop thinking about Ray, but it occurs to me that in some ways we are as close as brothers, as close as twins.

Even when we were not in communication with one another over all those years, we were tuned in to each-other's frequencies, so to speak, or so I liked to delude myself; but I don't know, finally, if I've ever had any influence at all on Ray. His effect on me has always been to produce exasperation. Although I've never really tried to sway his actions and decisions, I've always thought he ought to be able to exercise some control on his own. It's never worked out that way. From my distance, it appears that Ray's whole life has been governed by outside factors, that he's never succeeded in taking his destiny in hand to try to shape it as he wanted it to be.

Rather, he's gone with the flow, or with whatever tidal wave engulfed him at any particular moment. Perhaps what one can say about Ray is that he's a survivor, but I worry that simple survival may not be enough. There is also free will, and one ought to try, at least, to impose one's will upon the process of survival. At least so I would argue. Substituting accident, or the will of your wife, or what you perceive to be the will of the Lord for the determination you lack is too easy a way out of, or farther into, the morass of existence. I wonder if Ray will ever see that; I wonder if it's even true. Perhaps one day he'll get back in touch and tell me I'm wrong and that he's the happiest man on earth.

NANCY

One of the Reesatnafs was Carolyn Pearson. Of Swedish extraction, she was plump, blonde, sweet and Lutheran, none of which prevented her from incorporating into her personality senses of both sibling rivalry and mischief. The rivalry, and often the mischief, was directed toward her sister Dorothy, one year younger, equally pretty in a somewhat thinner, perter way.

I used to spend hours on the phone talking with various members of the Reesatnafs, Carolyn in particular. I preferred conversation to homework. On occasion these telephone marathons would begin to flag, the conversation wane into desultory comment wedged in between silences lengthening into the evening. When she and I were juniors and her sister a sophomore, Carolyn came up with a solution to this problem: she began sneaking Dorothy's diary out to the phone to read to me.

Our plot began with the discovery that Dorothy liked me while she was dating another Junior, Tomie DePaola, who, incidentally and coincidentally, had been my future wife Jean's closest childhood companion, playmate, and enemy. In a class full of remarkable people, Tomie eventually became perhaps the most famous. Even in high school he was an artist — as co-editor of the 1952 *Annual* I was his first publisher, for he was the Art Editor. Later on he went to Pratt Institute and turned himself into a children's illustrator, the author-illustrator of numerous picture storybooks. But even if one could have had a crystal ball, I doubt Tomie's glittering, if somewhat checkered, future would have cast a shadow on the conspiracy Carolyn and I hatched that evening.

We agreed that I would make a play for Dorothy to see if I could woo her away from Tomie. Carolyn was to keep me apprised of my progress by periodically reviewing with me over the phone her sister's recent entries. I didn't feel that the job would be onerous, as I rather liked Dorothy. So the campaign began.

It was immediately successful. I had only to listen to Dorothy's confessions as Carolyn read them into my ear each week, and I knew what to do and how things were going. Tomie never stood a chance. Soon he was cut out of the triangle and I had Dorothy to myself. No sooner was the goal won, though, than I began to chafe, for I had the habit of dating widely, which got for me a reputation, of which I was unaware, as a high school Lothario who loved 'em and left 'em.

How could I have worn such an aura? In those days when you dated around you were probably not doing a whole lot with anyone. I certainly wasn't, and for good reasons — my father being a preacher, I didn't want to cause him any problems in the community, even if I'd had the brass to attempt to do what I was assumed to be doing. Anyway, it was those people who went steady who were most likely to find themselves in trouble back in those dim days before The Pill, and I was going steady with no one.

Several years later, when her parents, sisters, and friends tried to talk Jean out of becoming engaged to me because I was sure to break her heart and maybe get her into trouble, I discovered with a deal of bitterness that I might as well have been doing what everyone assumed I had been. My chastity was invisible. Actuality is not as substantial as appearance — an early philosophical paradox; what is real is not as real as what is unreal. This is also an excellent principle of fiction writing, and I was eventually glad to have learned the lesson.

During high school I thought of The Reesatnafs as surrogate sisters, for I had none of my own. I never dated any of them, not even Jean until we had graduated and I was in the Navy. Paradox Number Two: sometimes people think, if they think of it at all, that paradox and oxymoron are rhetorical figures of speech, but life, especially in a small city, comes close to being such an anomaly, a closed circle, like Uroboros, the worm that feeds upon its own substance in order to renew itself.

Carolyn at least had no objection to or qualms about my dating Dorothy. One part of my reputation was deserved — I was fickle if not feckless. Nancy was a member of the mixed Special Chorus, Dorothy was not, and one Christmas Eve when the Chorus was involved in its annual pilgrimage of carols, I sat next to Nancy on the school bus. Although we'd been classmates for a year and a half, this was the first time I'd had anything to do with her, and I discovered that she was a great deal of fun. A Swede also, a Lutheran as well, even a member of the Emanuel Lutheran Church which Carolyn and Dorothy attended, Nancy lived on the Chamberlain Highway not far from my father's parsonage. We began walking to school across town together.

Then we began to double-date with her best friend Barbara Brooks — known to all as "Bobby"— and Bobby's boyfriend Paul Parks, a class ahead of us. I was callous enough to pick Nancy up one evening at the Lutheran church where she had been decorating the basement with Dorothy, among others, for some upcoming social function. I can bring to mind with a cringe the pleasured look Dorothy passed when she saw me walk in the door, and the stunned, hurt reproach in her eyes when I walked out with Nancy on my arm.

Perhaps I am committing an inexcusable blunder by admitting that I have never before or since experienced the kind of head-over-heels and heart-over-mind infatuation, delirium, obsession — call it what you will — that I felt for Nancy. She wasn't a particularly good-looking young woman: brown hair, blue eyes; thin, even to a degree gangly and angular, with a slight stoop. She was built nearly like a boy from the waist up; her teeth were crooked — Jean maintains to this day that they were "green," which I never noticed.

When I was with her, we were like two halves of a buffalo nickel spinning on its edge. All we had to do was hold hands, and my arms would tingle as though I had hold of both poles of a battery. We looked into each other's eyes and laughed for joy. Everything we attempted was more freshly alive, more fun than anything we'd ever done before without each other. We could talk about anything, get into any kind of mischief. I was deliriously happy. And I never laid a hand on her.

Perhaps that was the trouble because, Paradox Number Three, I was unfortunately also miserably unhappy. I have believed ever since that in every partnership one member has the upper hand. Depending on how that person exercises his or her power — that is, on the vagaries of personality — the relationship will float or founder.

Nancy loved to tease me. She knew exactly what to do not merely to hurt but to humiliate me. I despised myself for taking what I took from her, yet I was powerless to do anything other than accept it. In other words, she played what I now recognize to be the traditional male role, and I was reduced to the status of love slave, if such a symbiosis can be said to be love at all.

I remember one evening, coming back from a double-date with Bobby and Paul, Nancy and I sat in the back seat of the car. By the time we got to my house Nancy had good-naturedly cut me up so badly that I was bleeding from every pore. I managed to hide the fact, more or less, until I got to the back porch of the parsonage. I sat on the stairs, crossed my arms on my knees, put my head down and wept. My mother came out and asked me what was wrong and I told her, "Nothing." She looked on for a minute while I got control of myself, then she went back inside knowing full well what was wrong, if not in particular, at least in general.

I went upstairs to my room. It was summertime, June as I recall, though school was still in session. Nancy and I had been going steady for about six months, the longest I'd ever dated anyone. I sat down on the floor beside the low window, rested forearms and chin on the sill, and looked out at the Venice Restaurant across the street. The juke box was playing some tune of the nineteen-fifties, one of those songs that are already nostalgic while they're still on the pop-charts. It was one of the worst and saddest days of my life up to that point, if not the very saddest, which I think it was.

It was also the night, however, when I discovered to my great relief that there was alloy somewhere inside the wallowing emotional mush Nancy had made of a ridiculous adolescent boy. I decided while I listened to the sad songs of Tony Bennett and Nat Cole that the only way I could survive and begin liking myself again was to drop Nancy. A steel door shut in my mind. The next day I went to school and looked for Bobby. When I found her I said, "Tell Nancy it's over."

I can still see the incredulous stare she gave me. "Oh, come on," she said, "be serious! You tell her yourself." But I didn't trust myself that far, I just walked away.

And stayed away. Nancy didn't grovel or turn to blubber or anything like that, she just waited to see how long it was going to take for me to come around. Instead of doing so, however, I began to date again, and eventually I picked out a very pretty little sophomore, Marjorie, to go steady with. That lasted until I went into the Navy after graduation, at which point my new girlfriend dropped me, began going out with her best friend Gail's boyfriend, Jay, got pregnant, and got married. The next thing I heard was that Marjorie was dropping babies as though she were an assembly line. Annoyance was the strongest emotion I recall feeling in the case of these developments.

In the Navy I began to date Jean during the second year of my four-year hitch. She was attending the University of Connecticut and I was getting home frequently from Brooklyn where the new carrier *Hornet* was being readied for commission. I heard through the gossip mill that Nancy had gone somewhere to art school. Then the *Hornet* went to sea for six months, and Jean and I announced our engagement in *The Morning Record* and *The Journal*.

I was in the middle of the Pacific Ocean when I got Nancy's letter. It appeared to be written in eyebrow pencil in large script, or maybe that's just a figment of my recollection, my mind blowing up the event to larger than life size. She wrote that she'd seen the announcement of my engagement and couldn't believe her eyes. What in the world was the matter with me, picking out such a mouse as Jean? There was no one in the class who had less personality. If I were to persist in this amazing folly, I would be sure to regret it. What I wanted was someone who was "lively." That's the word she used, I remember clearly. I needed someone lively because I was myself a lively person. Lively and mousy could not co-exist.

That was as close as Nancy got to suggesting that we ought to get back together. I wrote her that I thought her letter was interesting, especially inasmuch as she had decided to enter the Navy herself when she had finished school. She had quit art and was planning to become a Navy nurse. This turn of events was never to be explained because I wrote a letter to end all further correspondence. I was offhand. I was debonair. I was totally in control — I told her about Japan, and how she would enjoy it if she ever got there. I even sent her a magazine article — from *The Atlantic*, as I recall — about Japan. My letter went on and on conversationally, meanly, teasingly.

I saved my *pièce de résistance* for last. I told her that I had been playing a lot of table tennis in port in Japan. Perhaps sometime soon, when I got back East, we could get together for a game or two of ping-pong. I would wager, I said, that "I can beat the pants off you, and you without your pants on I'd like to see." I loved the double entendre. It was witty and as nasty as I could make it.

That was the end of it, almost. To make a short story a bit longer, I spent two and a half more years as a yeoman in the Navy, all of them engaged to Jean while she finished her B.A. — her parents weren't about to pay her way through school if she married a sailor of dubious character. If I truly loved her I'd put up with the wait. They waited, too, very likely calculating that I'd never make it, but I did.

About the time I obtained my discharge, married my Reesatnaf, and spent the summer waiting to go to UConn myself by building houses with my seventh grade shop teacher *cum* father-in-law, Nancy went into the service as an ensign. Twenty-one years later I heard that she had never married, had retired as a Navy Commander, and was living in Virginia. In a fit of nostalgia I managed to track her down. I wrote to ask if she would be attending the twenty-fifth anniversary reunion of the class. She asked me to give her regards to Jean but said no, she didn't think she'd be able to make it.

Jean and I had made reservations for the dinner, but at the last minute I decided the car wasn't acting right, and I didn't want to chance a breakdown on the trip. There was no time to cancel, so our places remained empty at the banquet.

PETER THE UNLUCKY

Since we graduated from high school, Peter and I have kept in touch or, rather, he has. We never exchange letters — although I've written him, he's never written back. Instead, about once a year the phone will ring, and it will be Peter calling from California or wherever else he happens to be. In our high school yearbook *The Annual* for 1952 he is pictured with Carolyn Kamens among the class notables as "Most Likely to Succeed." Among the ads at the back of the book there's a snapshot of Peter standing in front of a blackboard. On the board there's a diagram and the caption reads, "The Peter Theorem," for the man has an I. Q. of 165.

Sometime during the fall of 1986 he phoned. "Luigi!" he said, "do you ever watch 'The Wheel of Fortune' on TV?"

I laughed. "Never. What's up?"

"Don't miss it tonight," he said, "tonight or tomorrow night — check your local listings. I'm on."

"Not again!" For Peter had been on a game show several years earlier, and he'd won quite a number of cash and prizes — but I'd missed that one. We chatted awhile.

"Do you have my new address?" he asked.

"I think so," I said, assuming he meant his second California address, though it wasn't that new. He asked if we'd be going back to Meriden for the Christmas holidays, but I said no, I had no family living there any more, and my wife Jean's sister Ann was the only member of her family still in town. "I'll be going to the Modern Language

Association convention in New York City just after Christmas, though, to help publicize *The New Book of Forms* which will just have been published."

"I'll be in the east then, too," he said. "Where will you be staying?"

"At the Grand Hyatt."

He said he'd probably catch me there. "Don't forget 'The Wheel of Fortune,'" he said.

I answered something like, "Okay, Peter, I'll make an effort to watch you tonight." But I did better than that. Even though I couldn't be home to see the program, I asked a colleague to tape the show for me, and not long afterward I bought a VCR myself. The tape became one of my fourteen-year-old son Christopher's favorite playbacks for a while. He kept bringing in friends to watch it.

The first contestant was Lee Stewart, a sailor; a secretary, Becky Edsel, was the second. Pat Sajak, the host, introduced "Peter" as "George." In fact, his first two names, like those of his late father, are George Peter, but when he was young everyone knew his father as George and no one called the son "junior," so he was called Peter instead. After the death of his father Peter began using his real first name, but I could never get used to it.

Sajak said that he saw my friend was a writer, and this seemed to take Peter aback. What I surmise is that he had said he was a "grants writer," someone who puts together proposals for foundation and government funding — Peter had been free-lancing along those lines for several years on the West Coast — and Sajak had misunderstood. In fact, Peter had wanted to be a writer, but he had never done anything with it. I'd been responsible for publishing a science-fiction poem of his in a little magazine called *Starlanes* back in the early 1950s, but I am unaware that he'd ever followed up with efforts of his own to appear in print. Whatever the case Peter, typically, blustered through Sajak's error and said he'd written some short stories and was working on a novel.

Peter was a good deal balder than when I'd seen him ten years or so earlier when he'd visited us in Oswego, New York, and brought us all a virulent, alien strain of flu. There was no mistaking him, however: the prominent aquiline nose set among the matching Greek features; the slightly stooped posture, which he righted now and again with a hitch of his shoulders thrown back; the satyr's grin, and the lively eyes darting shrewdly about. He looked newly showered and he was immaculately groomed.

My wife says her clearest recollection of Peter was at a party during high school at the home of our high school classmate and her childhood playmate, Tomie DePaola, now the famous children's writer and illustrator. She walked into a nearly-empty livingroom to see Peter standing before the mirror over the mantel, preening in the glass and admiring himself. "I remember thinking to myself, 'That's pure Peter,'" she told me.

When the preliminaries are over the sailor begins the game. He is looking to fill in a phrase, and on his first spin of the big wheel he asks for a "T." Vanna White turns over the appropriate square, and he gets his letter, but when he spins again the arrow lands on "Bankrupt," and it is the secretary's turn. She asks for an "H" on her first spin and gets two of them. The first word on the board is obviously "The." On her second spin she asks for an "R," but there is none in the phrase, and Peter gets to spin for the first time.

The arrow lands on $250.00 and Peter says with a big grimace, "I'd like an 'N'!" There are three of them in the phrase. He says, "I'll buy a vowel"— there are two E's in the phrase, including one in the first word, "The." On the next spin the arrow lands on $400.00 and Peter asks for an "S"— there are two of them; then "F": one word is obviously "of." Peter cannot lose — he spins again while the other two contestants look on with envy and boredom.

Next Peter wants an "M" and he gets two of them; "K" next — Peter has it. He says, "The milk of human kindness" in the carefully enunciating voice of an intelligent robot. Applause, applause — Peter, who has $2750.00, applauds himself and the audience does likewise. He shakes hands with Sajak.

When he came to visit us in Oswego where I had been teaching college for many years, we reminisced about our high school days and our crowd. I showed him that I still had a copy of our "Fantaseers" calling card: white lettering on black plastic, and a photo of the Fantaseers' Salem Witch Trials skit that I'd written and we'd performed in our junior year. There was Ben Barnes on the bench as judge Hathorne, holding up a string of paper dolls and cutting their heads off with a pair of scissors. I am dressed in my father's old swallow-tail coat, and Paul Wiese is the other prosecutor in an insane getup no Puritan ever wore. Peter is a member of the jury with the rest of the boys — Lindsey Churchill, Bill Burns, George Hangen, Art Von Au and the rest of them. Paul had wanted to gouge the eyes out of one of the witches, palm a hard-boiled egg, and throw it out into the audience, but the faculty censors — one was Mark Bollman, as I recall, and another, the Latin teacher, Ruth Coleman — wouldn't let us do it. Nevertheless, the production was a great success. Some of the girls in our crowd had played the witches.

Peter selects gold cufflinks as part of his prize, and "I've got to have that oak tray set for munchies," he says. Jean and I are groaning with chagrin as we sit in our living room before the television set. This is her first viewing, but I've returned to the tape time and again, fascinated as a cobra in a wicker basket listening to his fakir's piping. This is vintage Peter, the Attic pixy.

In high school Peter and Lindsey were known as the brains of the school. They were both members of the National Honor Society, both straight A students. Lindsey and I had been occasional playmates when

I'd lived on Curtis Street during the third and fourth grades at Israel Putnam School. The Churchills had lived on Elm Street, not far from the high school were Mr. Churchill taught English, and it was a considerable hike for me to Lindsey's house — I had no bicycle until the fifth grade. But we had gotten along well, though he was a year younger than I.

A year or two later Lindsey had skipped a grade, and in Meriden High during our sophomore and junior years, he was a member of our Class of 1952. Both he and Peter were charter members of the Fantaseers, our "Science Fiction Reading Club," the distaff side of which was the "Reesatnafs," of which my future wife was a peripheral member — peripheral in her own eyes, not in anyone else's. The combined bunch was "The Fantatnafs" — it was the girls who had coined that phrase.

Although Peter's I. Q. was well into genius range, Lindsey outstripped everyone at the end of our junior year by winning a full tuition scholarship to Yale University and skipping his senior year in high school. Peter was himself scheduled to attend Yale when he graduated. Although his classmates were well aware of Peter's brainpower, we also knew he was not as highly motivated as Lindsey, and we could hardly miss the fact that he tended to get through his courses with a minimum of effort and a maximum of glitter. Peter was nothing if not flashy in a sardonic sort of way.

Lee, the secretary, bends over to spin the Wheel of Fortune for her second try. She asks for a "T" — she is trying to figure out an event. She spins again and asks for an "H": there are two of them; spins again…and lands on "Bankrupt!" She loses her turn.

Back to Peter who spins, smiling. The arrow lands on $200.00 and he asks for an "R" — there are three in the event he's trying to guess. He elects to spin again; he calls out, "Pin! Pin! Pin!"and it does…the arrow lands on "Pin." He bends over the railing to pull the cover of the "Pin" space and discovers he has won only $150.00.

While we sat and talked during his visit to Oswego I was startled to hear Peter say, "I felt threatened by the Fantaseers."

"Threatened?" I asked.

"Yes. The Fantaseers seemed to be your milieu, but it was destabilizing for me. It wasn't the image I wanted. I wanted to be accepted by the athletes as well as the intellectuals, and the Fantaseers had the reputation of being oddballs."

"Then why did you belong?" I asked.

"Because all my non-jock friends belonged," he said.

He asks for an "N"— it begins to look as though his victory is assured. Vanna White turns over three N's on the board and Peter spins again. The arrow lands on $250.00 and Peter wants a "D" — the fourth word of the event is obviously "and." Peter wants an "A" and gets six of them!

Peter always wanted A's but, unfortunately, when he went to Yale he didn't get them. The glitter evidently wouldn't sustain him on the college level. While I was beginning my floating hegira about the world courtesy of the U. S. Navy, I heard that he'd had to leave Yale and, further, that he'd enrolled at New Britain State Teachers' College, now Central Connecticut State. I was amazed to learn eventually that he'd had no better luck there than at Yale.

Peter spins again, asks for an "L," gets two and elects to solve the puzzle for $1950.00: the event is, "Arriving an hour and a half late." Peter chooses a pocket watch for about $300.00, a chest for $435.00, an entertainment center for $1190.00 — after two rounds Peter has won $9275.00.

I'm not sure of the exact sequence of events that followed in Peter's early career. I know that he had to leave New Britain College a second time after being readmitted, and that he joined the Army and spent some time in Germany with the M.P.'s, but which came first I'm not sure. I do know that eventually, when he'd served his enlistment and returned to civilian life, he attended Fairfield University and acquired his B. A. at last. He was married.

Jean and I, and a friend, Marie, had dinner with the newlyweds one evening. Peter's bride served a dish I'd never had before but that I loved — hamburger Stroganoff. A year or two later their marriage was annulled — there were no children — and we were into the 1960s.

Jean and I had been married four years when, in 1960, our daughter Melora was born in Meriden during the summer between my leaving the University of Iowa Writers' Workshop and beginning my first teaching job at Fenn College. My *First Poems* was published the same summer. I'm not sure in what year Peter founded an "alternative school" for children in or around New Haven, but he stayed there awhile. Next we heard he'd gone to Cape Cod to be the founder of a similar public school program there. And then we pretty much lost track of what he was up to, though he'd fill in a few details when he put through his annual phone call.

Peter gets to spin first in the third round of "The Wheel of Fortune." The arrow lands on $400.00 and he asks for an "S" — there are two of them; he spins — $500.00 — asks for an "N" and gets it. He spins again: $250.00, asks for an "R"and gets two. Another spin, Peter asks for a "T" and gets one of those as well. He buys an "E" — there are three of them in the three words.

When my daughter Melora was about seventeen and my son, Christopher, four or five, Peter got married again. His bride was the daughter of a well-to-do New Jersey couple. Jean, and I went down to Meriden to visit our families, and we drove with Marie down to Jersey to the wedding. Unfortunately, we ran into a huge traffic jam on the Newburgh bridge along the route, and we arrived too late for the ceremony, but in time for the reception.

There we ran into several of our old high school classmates. One was Phil Riley who had lived nearly across the street from my family on North Third Street when I was in the fifth and sixth grades. Phil had a brother who was afflicted with Downs syndrome, and most of the neighborhood kids had been at least leery of him, if not downright afraid. Fortunately, these are more enlightened times. Jim Pagnam, also from the West Side unlike Peter, who was from the East Side of Meriden, was present as well, and one or two others including Jim Masterson. In high school Peter, like Lindsey, had been something of a jock as well as an intellectual, and these were more-or-less his jock friends rather than Fantaseers or Reesatnafs.

Peter wants another vowel, so he buys an "A" and Vanna White turns over the squares. He spins, the arrow lands on $900.00 this time! Peter wants a "P"— it's obvious now that the "thing" he is trying to guess is "Peppermint Life Savers," and Peter solves the problem. He applauds himself while Sajak celebrates his accomplishment. Peter selects his-and-her wedding bands and he says, "Okay, for $1800.00, let's go for the brass bed!" He says, "I'll take the books," and, with vast understatement, "I'm kind of a reader." He gets a stack of Simon and Schuster books, including the novel by John Erlichmann of Watergate infamy. Peter licks his lips as he listens to the list of all the things he's getting. He now has a total of $13,475.00 in money and prizes. We glimpse the sailor and the secretary out of the corner of the camera from time to time.

Peter worked for a New York publisher for a while as some sort of technical person having to do with the printing operation — or so I seem to remember, but that may have been earlier. He and Ceil moved out to California after a while and he began doing his grants writing for various colleges and institutions out there. I think, however, that eventually the Reagan administration cutbacks in support for science, health, and education seriously undermined Peter's ability to make a living by free-lancing, though Ceil always had a steady job.

This game-show program is practically a duplicate of the other that Peter had won not long after he began living on the west coast — it was, if I recall correctly, "Jeopardy" on that occasion. I hadn't seen it, but I heard that he'd won something like $40,000.00. Sajak wishes the sailor "Better luck next time" and thanks him and the silent secretary for being on the show. "It's a clean sweep for this guy," he says patting Peter on the shoulder.

Mugging away, Peter says, "Well, that's the way it goes." He says he's going to go for "The ca-a-ar!" — a Mazda RX7 sports car worth over $13,000.00. Peter has to guess a "Thing" in this portion of the show, which is a hurry-up version. He is given five consonants and a vowel, and he chooses "T, N, R, S, L," and "E." He gets the "L," the "N," two E's" — "Lead pencil" is the object. There is no way Peter can lose now. He solves the puzzle, and the audience goes bananas. Peter applauds too.

Pat Sajak takes the microphone off Peter, escorts him, with Vanna, to the car, and he gets in. Sajak says, "Look out, look like a winner, and wave to America." Peter hangs his head out the window, waves at the camera, and grimaces — it's supposed to be a smile, one surmises. He mugs away like crazy. Sajak says, "You know, back in the early days of television, there were a lot of kind of cerebral game shows with people like Bergen Evans and so forth...you look like a panelist on one of those shows."

Peter replies, "I would have been a panelist, but I ran out of wood." Sajak does a slow double take, mutters something half under his breath, says goodbye to the audience, and the game is over. Peter has won everything, over $32,000.00 in all.

That was in 1986. Four or five years later Peter put through his annual call, but he acted a bit oddly on the phone. When I tried to call him back at home I got Ceil who seemed startled. She said he wasn't there, and she gave me another number to call. When I got Peter back on the line he admitted that he'd phoned to ask for a loan but had chickened out. He and his wife had split up and he'd been living in an apartment with several other men. He was afraid he was going to be out on the street if he didn't get up his portion of the rent.

"But what happened to the money you won on 'Wheel of Fortune'? I asked. Ah, he said, that had gone to pay the back taxes on the things he'd won on "Jeopardy" — the IRS had hounded him for years. I told him I'd send him a fair amount to help him out. He said he'd pay me back one day, but I told him not to worry about it.

A year or so later he phoned again. The touch was easier this time, it seemed. "I can't afford to adopt you, Peter," I said. He argued with me, but I refused. "I already have a family," I told him. "You have one too, don't you?"

"Yeah, if you can call them that," he said.

"I've already sent you a rather large sum of money on one occasion," I told him.

"Oh, yeah. That came in handy," he said.

Some time later he called once more. This time all he wanted was a small loan — he said he was living out of his car. I told him that what he wanted from me wouldn't solve his problem, nor even stave it off for long. There were social agencies in San Francisco that could do him some permanent good, so I refused again and he rang off in anger. Since then I have received one or two collect calls from San Francisco, but the caller on each occasion has hung up before I could accept. "You will not be charged for this call," the operator informed me.

In July of 1994, at a reunion of the old high school crowd that was held on Cape Cod in the home of Carolyn, one of the Reesatnafs, I discovered that Peter at one time or another had also phoned several of those who were present to request money, which some of them had sent. "You know, we saw him several times when he was working with his alternative school in Barnstable," Carolyn said. She told us that when Peter had called her from the West Coast to ask for a loan, it had coincidentally been on the evening that some friends of hers and her husband's had been visiting from San Francisco. When Peter had hung up Carolyn explained the situation to her guests, one of whom was herself a worker in the San Francisco social services system. She promised that when they got home she would try to locate Peter and give him a hand. "She did try," Carolyn said, "but she could never locate him anywhere."

On another visit to Meriden some time later I was discussing Peter with Jim Masterson. "You know what his problem is, don't you?" he asked me.

"Not really."

"He's an addict."

I was astonished. "I never saw Peter take drugs, though I've seen him drink some."

Jim shook his head. "Not drugs or alcohol," he said.

"What, then?"

"Gambling."

I cast my mind back to the early years, and I recollected that Peter had always been involved in poker games, at Fantaseer meetings, at parties, after school, even during study halls sometimes.

"That's why he never went to class in college," Jim said. "All he did was play cards. That's what happened to the money he won on those game shows, all the money his friends sent him. Sometimes he was lucky, most times he was not."

And that's what luck can do to a guy with an I. Q. of 165.

JEAN

I knew who Jean was three years before she knew who I was. I can actually recall the moment I saw my future wife for the first time. I was standing with a friend — I think it was Jackie Maier — in the driveway of Lincoln Junior High School, in Meriden, Connecticut. It was located near the corner of West Main Street where Windsor Avenue turns into North Third Street. The year was 1946, the month September. Jackie and I had been classmates during the fifth and sixth grades at Benjamin Franklin School farther up West Main, and now we were attending the seventh grade together. If the day were not in fact the first day of the fall term, then it was an early day.

While we stood looking toward the school a pretty girl came out of the side door and walked along the building toward the street. "Who's that?" I asked and pointed.

"Boy, stay away from her! That's old man Houdlette's daughter," Jackie said. I knew who Mr. Houdlette was, for I was a member of his shop class. Mr. Houdlette terrified me, as he terrified all the boys, for he was the disciplinarian of the school as well as the woodworking instructor. "I wouldn't want to be her," Jackie went on. "Every night when she gets home he beats her." I made a mental note to stay as far away from Jean Houdlette as possible.

At the beginning of the first woodworking class Mr. Houdlette had called us to order outside the "cage" where most of the portable lethal tools were kept locked up. "It's important that you do exactly as I say," he said, "because the shop is a dangerous place." He pointed to a bunch of leather straps hanging to the wire grillwork on the inside of the cage. "Do you see those straps?" he asked. "I use those on boys who disobey me. I have to," he said solemnly. He pointed in another direction. "Do you see that machine? That's a band-saw. Let's say you didn't do exactly as I say when you use that machine and you ran your hand through the blade instead of a stick of wood." He paused significantly. "Why, if you hurt yourself, I'd feel all cut up about it...and so would you!"

There was a peculiar pause during which conflicting emotions and sensations ran through my nerve cells and my brain. Mr. Houdlette was grinning. I doubt I knew the word at the time, but it seemed clear to me that he was what I would later understand to be a Sadist. Jackie Maier's description of Mr. Houdlette and the fate of his daughter were credible to me under the circumstances. I felt great pity for Jean, but I was in no position to save her.

That scene in front of the cage sticks in my mind for a reason other than the threat Mr. Houdlette laid on us: it was the first time I was consciously aware of hearing a pun. I knew about puns, though, for I had recognized one in a comic book years earlier, when I was in the second grade at Roger Sherman School and we were living for a year or so on Newton Street on the east side of town. In the first panel a comic character asks another, "How are you feeling today?"

The second figure replies, "I'm feeling pony."

"How's that?"

"A little hoarse."

As soon as I heard Mr. Houdlette's pun and looked around me at the stricken faces of my fellow apprentices, I believe I understood the essential perversity of this form of humor. Though I would always be wary of violent behavior and would go a long way to avoid it, from that moment forward I embraced the pun — indeed, I would often use it thereafter to avoid violence by baffling and confusing an opponent until I could find a way out of the confrontation. It didn't always work, but often it did. It was a good lesson for a future writer to learn, that the tongue can be sharper than the teeth of a band saw.

I lay low in Mr. Houdlette's class from that moment forward — so low, in fact, that in later years he had no recollection at all of me as one of his pupils, though he remembered my younger and much quieter brother Gene who followed in my footsteps through Lincoln five years later. I recall I made a tie rack in shop that semester, with beveled edges and a pine stain.

The next term — my last at Lincoln — I took printing with Jack Conroy, Mr. Houdlette's old friend and his neighbor on Highland Avenue. The two of them and a third teacher, Joseph Nadile, had, before the war, built their three houses side by side, using only each-other's labor. It had been the depression, and local carpenters had picketed them, but I gather they'd done so with little conviction, for the teachers weren't actually hiring anyone to work, after all.

Jack had gone off to the War when it began, and he had only recently returned from Europe where he had served in the Army. All the boys looked up to him as the next thing to a hero, if he weren't one in fact, and nobody feared him, but we all would do anything he asked. He needed no threats. I liked printing better than woodworking, but I can't recall what it was I produced in his class, which was held in the rear of the same shop where woodworking was taught.

The year ended, the summer passed, and I returned to Lincoln the following fall only briefly, for I was to attend Suffield Academy in Suffield, Connecticut, up between Hartford and Springfield, Massachusetts. My father was sending me there, I learned years later, "...to save my life," as Gene put it to me in middle age, a notion that astonished me, for I'd been led to believe at the time that Suffield was a great privilege, a financial sacrifice my parents were making in order to give me the best possible boost into the world of adulthood. Besides, though I was pretty mean to him in a standard, big-brotherly kind of way, I never intended to maim Gene permanently. He learned to do quite a good job of that on his own, what with catching poison ivy all over his body after he walked through the smoke of a bonfire; holding firecrackers too long in his hand, and firing a BB pellet that ricocheted off the garage door and split his cornea. It's a miracle he — or either one of us, or any boy, for that matter — survived childhood.

I think the worst thing I ever did to Gene was tie him to the porch when my parents went off somewhere for a while and left me to baby-sit him. I didn't want to be tied down myself, so I made sure he was safe and then hunted up the gang on Windsor Avenue to fool around with. I recall Gene yelled and cried a lot, but as long as I could hear him I knew he was okay.

There's empirical evidence, now that I think of it, to support Gene's claim that I was being shipped away to save wear and tear on the family, for I'm certain my father sent me to spend the first two weeks of the fall term in Lincoln because he couldn't stand to have me around the house while all the rest of the local kids were in school and we were waiting for the term at Suffield to begin in mid-month. He didn't realize it, but sending me to Lincoln was a mistake, for I had nothing to lose there. In the halls I soon met my boon companion Paul, a hellion greater than I, and together we reduced authority to powder — even Mr. Houdlette's. Miraculously, we got away with it. At least I did.

The two years I spent at Suffield were different from anything I was exposed to prior to the Navy, and the constant supervision produced in me an honor roll student on most occasions. The eighth grade was the third year of Lower School, which was comprised also of the sixth and seventh grades. We boys lived in an old wooden-frame dormitory set off from the Upper School buildings, immediately behind the town library which did double service as the school library. I learned the ropes well enough that first year to decide, at the beginning of freshman year of Upper School, to try my hand at politics. I walked around glad-handing

Fantaseers

everyone, smiling a lot, being everybody's pal, and got myself elected Class President. It was so easy that I have scorned politics ever since. A politician is nothing but a classier caliber of used car salesman.

At the end of my freshman year my father's money ran out and I had to return to Meriden to attend high school. One might think I'd have been used to changing schools every year or two, for my family had moved into nearly every quarter of town before the church had purchased a parsonage next door to it, on the corner of Windsor and Springdale, just before my seventh-grade year at Lincoln. I'd spent only one full year in the house, and now I was to leave the boarding-school environment, to which I'd become acclimated if not completely attached; I was once more to be torn from all my friends and classmates to attend a strange school where, without a doubt, I would know no one and would once more have to struggle to make my place. This was not a good example of clear thinking, but it's what I believed.

When I got home I saw an opportunity to make my presence known to the town, my future classmates, and my new teachers before school even began. A local paper — was it *The Morning Record* or the *Journal*? — announced concurrent short-story contests for junior high and high school students during the summer, and I entered. When the results were announced, I had won third prize in the high school category with a piece whose title I can no longer remember, but I rewrote it many times and eventually cannibalized it for another story published years later, "Shipmates," most recently included in my *The Book of Dialogue* in 2004. The original version appeared in the paper during the summer of 1949, and I felt a little better about people knowing who I was when the fall term began.

At last the much-anticipated and worrisome day arrived. I walked across town, west to east, to Meriden High for the first time with one of my friends from Windsor Avenue, Alle Lamphier, whom I'd known and played with since the seventh grade. He was some comfort.

We climbed the hill to the school, we climbed the long flight of stairs, and we paused halfway up. I looked about with trepidation, but my expression must have changed from worry to amazement and then to joy — for, far from finding myself in an enormous crowd of strangers, I knew everyone! Or so it seemed. Here were all my playmates, classmates, and friends from all the neighborhoods my family had lived in during a period of more than a decade, gathered in one spot.

Paul Wiese from South Meriden was there, in my homeroom with Alle Lamphier, Jack Maier, Curt Offen, Lindsey Churchill (whose father taught English in the high school) and dozens of others from Benjamin Franklin, Roger Sherman, Israel Putnam, and Lincoln Junior High schools; from Lewis, Windsor, and Springdale avenues; Prospect, Curtis, Newton, and North Third streets. There were even people from my Sunday School classes and my church!

My god! It was a convention of cohorts, a panoply of playmates, a midden of merrymakers: Marie Delemarre, whose father ran a candy shop on Liberty Street when I was in the third grade; big Barbara Little, from the fifth grade, still taller than I was; Mary Lou Burke, my girlfriend in the seventh grade (or so I thought of her, since she had been my first "date" — we'd gone to the movies together with a gang of kids), Janice Allaire (the one I'd really wanted to go to the movies with, but she was the private property of Tom Chiovolone, in his opinion), Marie Cantarini from church...and Jean Houdlette (who didn't know me, but I knew her).

I no longer had to worry about her father, all I had to do was worry about rejection, for she was both beautiful and quiet. The looks intimidated me, and her silence I interpreted as hauteur rather than the shyness it actually was. With Jean I immediately fell into an adversarial relationship in self-defense, but for the rest of it, I went mad! All the discipline I'd learned at Suffield went out the window. Paul and I immediately resumed the manic behavior we had shared briefly at

Lincoln. Among the teachers my short story had some effect, and perhaps it also had an effect among those young people I'd not known elsewhere, but I didn't need its fame, for I was immediately one of the best-known members of the Class of 1952.

Soon I had added to my list of friends all the young men in my homeroom, including Ray Staszewski and Greg, and all the people in the many clubs I joined — the Special Chorus, which broke down into the Men's Glee Club, and then an octet, and ultimately into a foursome, the Sportlanders Barbershop Quartet. Soon a group of us found we were science-fiction readers, and we formed The Fantaseers with its women's auxiliary, The Reesatnafs, of which Jean was a member.

I took to following her down the hill after school as we began the mile-long trek across town to our homes. I dropped jibes upon her rigid back. I kidded her and ribbed her and thought I was being the cleverest fellow in the world — nowadays it would probably be called "sexual harrassment." I suppose I thought this was a way of winning her attention if not her admiration. I never realized that tears were running down the cheeks she kept averted from me, under that crown of light brown, nearly blonde hair — I wonder if I fell in love with her because of the song I'd heard as a child and always felt wistful about, or whether it was her status as the forbidden fruit, or just because I thought she was too good for me and wanted her therefore.

But we never dated in high school. I went out with gaggles of girls. I never did anything beyond heavy petting with any of them, and that is the truth, but my reputation — if only I had known it at the time! — was one of the worst in the school. People assumed that I was running amok among the blushing maidens, but you can't run amok if you date a girl only once or twice. Even my "steady" girls generally lasted no more than a month or two. I spent half my poor pay from Kresge's Five and Ten Cent Store on ID bracelets. Jack Golab at his jewelry shop down by the Palace Theater, across from Katt Brothers and Paul's father's Butter and Egg Store, just loved to see me coming.

When my class graduated and I joined the Navy with my classmate Ray, I broke up with Marge Young, my last high school steady. A year later Jean and I began dating somehow, after a party. I'd come up for a weekend from Brooklyn Naval Shipyard where my carrier, the *Hornet*, was being commissioned, and I'd run into Jean. I cornered her and began talking with her, face to face, I think really for the first time. She didn't move away. She smiled. I dared ask her out.

Not a great while later — about six months, as I recall — I took her to dinner at the Chinese restaurant in Meriden. It was located on the second floor, over some shops across East Main Street from the railroad station. I was still wary of rejection, so I had put some thought into how I was going to phrase my proposal over my favorite meal there, breaded veal cutlets — I don't know why a Chinese restaurant would serve such a dish. It is one of the many small mysteries of a lifetime.

"If I bought you a ring, would you wear it?" I asked.

"Yes," she said.

Afterward, I took Jean home and she told her mother what I'd said. "Oh, Jean" she groaned. "Do you realize what you've done?"

"What?" Jean asked.

"He's asked you to marry him. You're engaged!"

Jean tells me she thought it over and wasn't surprised.

"But what about your college?" Mrs. Houdlette asked — Jean had just finished her freshman year at the University of Connecticut in Storrs.

Her sister Ann said, "Oh, no! He's got the worst reputation in town!" Ann had eloped with a flyer during the War at the age of sixteen and found herself a widow with a baby a year later.

"He's a hellion," her sister Nathalie said with some temper.

Some temper — a good match for that of her sometime Irish-American husband Larry.

"Isn't his father that Italian preacher?" her sister Betty asked. She was married to a chap named "Falton," né "Faltonovich."

I went back to Jack Golab's shop. "What!" he said. "Another I.D. bracelet?"

"It'll be a diamond this time, Jack. Show me what you've got in a wedding set."

Jean and I were engaged two and a half years while I took a world cruise. We were married two weeks before my discharge from the Navy, and a month after Jean's graduation from college in 1956.

During that summer before I, too, entered UConn (on a scholarship from the *Record*), I worked with Jack Conroy and John Houdlette building two houses for which my father-in-law had contracted, for he had recently retired from teaching. "Lew isn't much on finish work," he told Jean, "but he's all right on framing and rough work."

One might have predicted, I suppose, that Dad Houdlette would turn out to be the kindest man, other than my own father, I have met in my life. Although in his youth he was reputed to have been himself a hellion in school, and in his young manhood he had a hot temper, he had never in her life laid a hand on his youngest daughter, though that claim could not be made in the cases of the elder three.

I remember one scene in particular from that summer. We were building a house in Yalesville, not far from Meriden. Jean's father and I were up on the roof putting down shingles when Jack came along and borrowed our ladder. The sun was out, but it wasn't unpleasant. While we worked, Dad kept up a steady commentary on this, that, and everything in his pleasant Maine accent. He loved to fool around with words, though he was no writer. His favorite author was Joseph C. Lincoln. He used phrases like "garp and swaller" for frothy edibles, and words like "gumshalloobie" for glue or sticky stuff. His preferred curse, when he couldn't stand it anymore, was "Jesus to Jesus and eight hands 'round!"

When we were through on the roof and wanted to get down I called to Jack to bring the ladder back. He grabbed it, hoisted it straight up into the air, and headed for me on the eaves, but he detoured and then began walking in a circle, still carrying his burden. "What the hell are you doing, Jack?" I asked.

"Nothin' much," he said. "I'm just one of the ladder day saints."

"Good grief," I said. "Did you ever hear that 'all cut up' pun of Dad's?"

"Oh, sure," Jack said, setting the ladder against the house. "He used to use it every term."

"Well, the sun's going down and I'm feeling pony," I told him.

"How's that?"

"A little hoarse."

"Maybe you've caught a colt," he said.

"Jesus to Jesus and eight hands 'round!" said Dad who'd been listening.

"Poor Jean!" say all our friends, shaking their heads. "How long have you had to put up with this?"

"Over fifty years," she tells them these days. But it isn't all my fault. I had wonderful teachers.

Lew & Jean Turco, 1953

LEWIS TURCO
at the 2004 West Chester Poetry Conference
photo credit: Robert Ward

— *About the Author*

In 2004 Star Cloud Press of Scottsdale, Arizona, published both *A Sheaf of Leaves: Literary Memoirs* and *The Collected Lyrics of Lewis Turco / Wesli Court,* two of the most recent books by Lewis Turco, who was the founding director of both the Cleveland State University Poetry Center, in 1962, and of the Program in Writing Arts at the State University of New York, from 1968 through 1995. He is the author of some 44 books, monographs and chapbooks including *The Book of Forms: A Handbook of Poetics* (1968); *Awaken, Bells Falling: Poems 1959-1968* (1968); *The New Book of Forms* (1986); *Visions and Revisions of American Poetry* (winner of the Poetry Society of America's 1986 Melville Cane Award for literary criticism); *The Shifting Web: New and Selected Poems* (1989), *The Public Poet: Five Lectures on the Art and Craft of Poetry* (1991); and *Emily Dickinson: Woman of Letters, Poems and Centos from Lines in Emily Dickinson's Letters* (1993). He was the 1997 winner, with his Italian translator Joseph Alessia, of the first annual Bordighera Bilingual Poetry Prize for his *A Book of Fears* (1998); a chapbook of memoirs, *Shaking the Family Tree,* was published simultaneously.

The Book of Literary Terms, The Genres of Fiction, Drama, Nonfiction, Criticism and Scholarship was published in 1999 and was cited by *Choice* as an Outstanding Academic Title for the year 2000. In the latter year a companion volume, the third edition of *The Book of Forms, A*

Handbook of Poetics was published, and in 2004 a third volume in the series was published, *The Book of Dialogue,* all by the University Press of New England.

Mr. Turco has collaborated with various artists over the years. At S.U.N.Y. Oswego the poet collaborated first in 1966 with the printmaker Thom. Seawell in three poemprints. Their final collaboration was on a book, *The Inhabitant,* poems, with prints by Thom. Seawell, including the inspiration for the book a fold-out reproduction of a huge woodcut, "The House," by Seawell, both projects funded by summer Faculty Fellowships from the Research Foundation of State University of New York. The book was published by Despa Press in 1970. "While the Spider Slept," a ballet based upon his poem "November 22, 1963," choreographed by Brian Macdonald with music by Maurice Karkoff, was performed in 1968 and subsequently by the Royal Swedish Ballet and the Royal Winnipeg Ballet. With the Dutch composer Walter Hekster (who is married to a Reesatnaf, Alice Van Leuvan) Lewis Turco wrote and published a chamber opera, *The Fog* (Donemus, 1987).

Four Turco poems from two short collections, *A Family Album* (1990), winner of the Silverfish Review Chapbook Award, and *Murmurs in the Walls* (1992), winner of the Cooper House Chapbook Award, appeared in national juried art and poetry exhibits mounted by the Peconic Gallery of Riverhead, Long Island, New York. The complete series of these poems, *The Green Maces of Autumn: Voices in an Old Maine House,* was published in 2000 by the Mathom Bookshop. His *Bordello: PoemPrints,* a portfolio with collaborator printmaker George O'Connell, was published during a debut exhibition from April 11 to May 12, 1996, at The Rathbone Gallery in Albany, New York. Another collaboration, "The Jazz Joint," was included in a four-person show, "Some Kind of Narrative," at the Kirkland (New York) Art Center during March 2001. "Collaboration: Poems by Lewis Turco, Prints by George O'Connell, A Retrospective 1981-2001" opened at the Tyler Art Gallery at Oswego State University on October 13, 2001 and ran for one month.

Lewis Turco took the B. A. from the University of Connecticut in 1959 and the M. A. from the University of Iowa in 1962. In 1992 he received a Distinguished Alumnus Award from the Alumni Association of the University of Connecticut; he was inducted into the Meriden, Connecticut, Hall of Fame in 1993, and in 1999 he received the John Ciardi Award for lifetime achievement in poetry sponsored by the periodical *Italian Americana* and the National Italian American Foundation. In May 2000 Mr. Turco received an honorary degree, Doctor of Humane Letters, from Ashland University in Ohio. In June 2004 he was honored with a panel and gave a reading at the West Chester University Poetry Conference in Pennsylvania where the book *Lewis Turco and His Work: A Celebration,* edited by Steven E. Swerdfeger, was published by Star Cloud Press. He is listed in *Who's Who in America* and in *The Encyclopedia of American Literature* among other reference works.

Jean Houdlette and Tomie DePaola in a play at
Meriden High School, 1951

The Fantaseers' Salem Witchcraft Skit, 1951

Lewis Turco, 1952 Graduation Photo

Fantatnafs in later years: Jean Turco, Lewis Turco,
Alice Van Leuvan Hekster, Walter Hekster, and Marie Delemarre Ho.